New Monetarism

by

David Roche and Bob McKee

The authors

David Roche is President and chief global strategist of Independent Strategy, a global investment consultancy based in London, Hong Kong and Zurich. He has worked in the investment business for over 30 years and was formerly global strategist for Morgan Stanley before founding Independent Strategy. He has been particularly acclaimed for predicting the Fall of the Wall and the end of the Soviet era in the 1980s; the emergence of global disinflation in 1990s with purchasing power going from corporations to the people; and for forecasting the Asian financial crash of 1997-8. In 2006, he developed the theory of New Monetarism that predicted the global credit crunch. Irish, he lives in Hong Kong with his three wild dogs.

Bob McKee is chief economist at Independent Strategy. He has also worked in the investment business for decades and was formerly part of David Roche's global strategy team at Morgan Stanley. Like David, he is a regular contributor to business broadcasting including TV with CNBC, BBC, Bloomberg etc as well as for various printed journals. He worked with David in developing the theory of New Monetarism and its prediction of the credit crunch. He is British and lives in London.

Contents

Preface to the 2<u>nd</u> edition

It is now nearly one year since the global credit crunch broke out in August 2007. We've run out of copies of the first edition. So we've taken the opportunity to produce a new edition with updated data. We've also included a new chapter that looks at the world after the credit crisis and considers how to invest in it.

July 2008

The great serendipity

Liquidity may be the most overused word in the financial lexicon but it is among the most meaningful for asset prices. No one watching the electric action of financial markets in spring and summer 2007 can have any doubt that, when the quantity and cost of money available for investment changes or when risk appetite to lend or borrow it shifts, asset markets can freeze to the point of threatening the global financial system.

This short book tells how and why this happens. It defines 'liquidity' and describes how its changing nature in recent decades makes it a more vital concept for investors than the so-called 'real' economy that produces all the goods and services we use in our daily lives. We shall share with you the tools we use to match investment strategy with the liquidity cycle.

In the old days the economic cycle set the tone of financial markets. Now with global liquidity valued at nearly twelve times that of GDP, the current of causality runs the other way (Figure 1). As often as not, financial markets set the tone of the real economy. How this came to be and how it works are captured by our theory of New Monetarism.

New Monetarism describes a set of economic conditions that for two decades allowed for the creation of massive liquidity without engendering high inflation in goods and services or a high cost of capital. Instead,

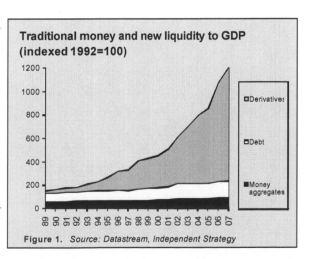

Traditional money and new liquidity to GDP (indexed 1992=100)

☐Derivatives

☐Debt

■Money aggregates

Figure 1. *Source: Datastream, Independent Strategy*

the value of financial assets grew far faster than the underlying economy.

From the early 1980s sane central bank policies, globalisation and technologies such as the internet allied to reduce inflation progressively. Lower inflation meant cheap money. Lots of it was created and in many new forms, most dedicated to investing rather than shopping. Because of this, and the new supply of cheap goods and services over the internet and from China, increased liquidity did not result in inflation in the shops, but in asset prices.

At the same time, lower inflation put a stop to 'stop-go' economic cycles. Economies went on expanding steadily for very long periods of time. As a result, the 'volatility' of the macro economy fell. This meant that growth; jobs, wages and profits were also much less volatile than before. This phenomenon is known as The Great Moderation. All of these factors together are the great serendipidity that allowed New Monetarism to exist. New Monetarism is not so much a new paradigm as the result of propitious economic circumstances and thus will last for only as long as they do.

Is New Monetarism good or bad news for the world economy and people's wealth? Liquidity like beauty can be virtuous or evil. On the one hand, the world needs liquidity to make the wheels of wealth and of the global economy rotate. Too little and the wheels will grind to a halt.

The new forms of liquidity under New Monetarism have increased the shock absorption capacity of markets by decreasing financial market volatility and spreading financial risk better. They have provided a new insurance function against changes in interest rates or default in traditional debt markets. But New Monetarism also makes the financial sector much more vulnerable to liquidity shocks, which is now an even bigger risk than insolvency — the normal measure used to judge the soundness of financial institutions.

Nevertheless, up until August 2007, New Monetarism contributed to increased confidence and lower volatility in asset prices. Banks and corporations thus felt comfortable in increasing the lending and leverage relative to reserves and equity.

But the positive impacts of such financial engineering (risk absorption capacity) can also encourage excessive risk taking, lending and borrowing based on 'flat world' faith. Flat world faith is a sense of false confidence that the superlative financial engineering of New Monetarism has ended economic and financial cycles.

This faith affects human behaviour. If a businesswoman believes that profits and the cost of money will never change, she will borrow and invest more than if she is uncertain about these factors in the future. This confidence opens the way for high levels of liquidity creation (the fruit of excess borrowing and lending). But it also means severe liquidity contraction, when all is reversed.

For that to happen, the quantity of liquidity has to shrink or its price has to rise or the willingness to lend and borrow has to fall. And because financial assets and wealth are now valued so much more than the real economy, the spill-over effect will be felt in the global economy soon.

For this, do not blame New Monetarism or the financial engineering of new financial markets. It is down to how people use these financial instruments. To map how to cope with this uncertain future and protect wealth is the purpose of this book.

And if you want a more light-hearted look at how New Monetarism has worked for good and ill, read our final chapter on the story of Coconut Island.

CHAPTER ONE

New Monetarism and disinflation

Our story starts with the last 25 years of disinflation. What is disinflation? It is years of falling price increases, but not (in a generalised sense) falling prices. That would be deflation, not disinflation.

From about 1982, global price increases slowed year after year. This disinflation was caused by several factors.

First, sane central bankers started to target low inflation as a priority for monetary policy. Second, globalisation empowered producers of cheap things, like China, to sell their wares to rich folk without too much interference from protectionist tariffs or quotas.

Third, the internet created competition in consumer markets and so shifted pricing power away from producers to the people.

Fourth, the internet also made it easier for companies to manage global supply chains more efficiently.

And finally, governments acted to empower markets rather than strangle them and also limit their own spending and deficits.

Most of the improvement in inflation came early in the disinflationary period (Figure 2). Thereafter, inflation marked time, but at a sustained low level.

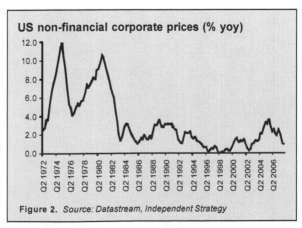

US non-financial corporate prices (% yoy)

Figure 2. *Source: Datastream, Independent Strategy*

NEW MONETARISM AND DISINFLATION

In the 1980s, the battle against inflation was fought (and won) by central bankers. So beating inflation was a monetary phenomenon.

Only subsequently in the 1990s did Chinese production and the spread of the internet keep prices low.

Indeed, at first, the bond market didn't believe that inflation was licked for a very long time after it was. That's because inflationary expectations had been set by monetary and fiscal policies in the first 25 years after the second world war. So investors were reluctant to buy bonds in the early years of disinflation because they just didn't believe that lower inflation would last.

As a result, bond yields stayed high in real terms (after inflation is deducted) and declined only gradually as investor expectations adjusted to the new disinflationary world.

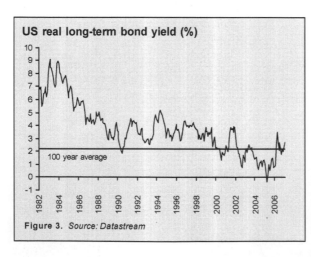

Figure 3. *Source: Datastream*

By the time the disinflationary period ended around 2004-5 the real cost of long-term debt was way below its long-term average (Figure 3), or what could be considered the 'natural rate' that equates supply of capital with productive investment.

Inflation began to return to the global economy since 2004, if only moderately. But bond markets still seem to expect inflation to be low forever and real yields remain low historically. Perhaps this represents the same lag in the adjustment of inflationary expectations to underlying reality as at the beginning of the disinflationary decades, but now operating in reverse.

Disinflation's double whammy

Disinflation made us all rich. All asset prices rose in relation to their income. That's because disinflation gave us lower inflation and a lower real cost of capital. The combination made every dollar earned in the future worth more today.

So capitalisation rates rose: the value of every asset, from houses to equities, rose faster than the income each could (potentially) generate. Viewed another way, familiar to equity investors, the asset price multiple (think of it as sort of a giant P/E of the whole economy), judged by the value of capital used to produce all output, jumped up in a step change.

Disinflation also helped corporate managers to make higher profits by keeping wage costs (under pressure from China's 'boundless' cheap labour) down. Lower inflation also meant corporations could make better long-term investment decisions. After all, how long is your investment horizon if inflation is 100% or higher, making all profits worthless after a year?

So, during the disinflationary decades, corporations saw the E in P/E grow fast, while the P was expanding even faster. That is the secret of disinflation's double wealth whammy. It boosted income. But it also hefted the present value or price that investors were willing to pay to get that income.

Of the two wealth effects, the biggest was the effect of lower inflation and higher capitalisation rates on asset prices. For US equities, during the disinflationary decades, rising P/Es accounted for two-thirds of total re-

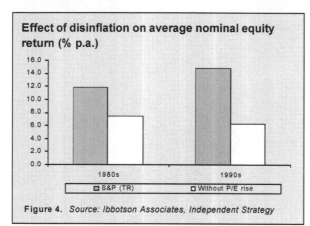

Effect of disinflation on average nominal equity return (% p.a.)

Figure 4. *Source: Ibbotson Associates, Independent Strategy*

turns in equity markets and rising corporate profits only one-third (Figure 4).

Moreover, the price of 'unproductive' real estate rose even more relative to rent than the price of equity in the (presumably) 'productive' corporate sector increased relative to profits.

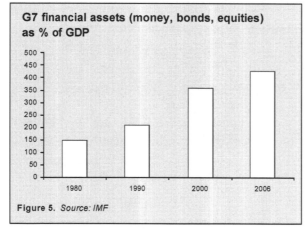

G7 financial assets (money, bonds, equities) as % of GDP

Figure 5. *Source: IMF*

So people got wealthier from rising asset values. And they got wealthier way faster than from rising GDP, profits or rents (Figure 5).

But wealth can grow faster than GDP only if some or all of three things are in place.

First, the share of profits (the income assets earn) in GDP must expand. It did throughout the disinflationary years because the wage share was compressed (Figure 6).

This didn't make workers too unhappy because wages were also growing (albeit not as fast as GDP) and globalisation of trade was making things cheaper for workers to buy. So workers got richer in real terms, if not

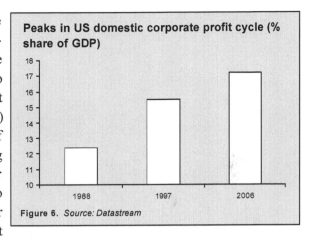

Figure 6. *Source: Datastream*

as quickly as the owners of capital (although they were increasingly the same people through participation in pension funds, retirement accounts, mutual funds etc).

Wealth can also grow faster than GDP if inflation shifts permanently to a lower plane and/or (often as a result) the cost of capital does. As we described above, this boosts asset values relative to income or GDP (national income).

And finally, wealth can rise faster than GDP if there is enough of the right type of money around to fund rising asset values and output without driving up inflation for goods and services.

New Monetarism enters stage left!

This is where New Monetarism enters the stage. This was the other major reason why, during disinflation, financial assets grew much more in value than GDP or than any 'material' economic activity underpinning asset values.

NEW MONETARISM AND DISINFLATION

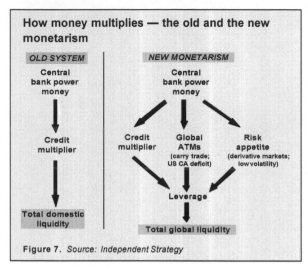

How money multiplies — the old and the new monetarism

OLD SYSTEM

Central bank power money

Credit multiplier

Total domestic liquidity

NEW MONETARISM

Central bank power money

Credit multiplier

Global ATMs
(carry trade; US CA deficit)

Risk appetite
(derivative markets; low volatility)

Leverage

Total global liquidity

Figure 7. *Source: Independent Strategy*

Rising financial asset prices was partly the result of the better mobilisation of existing credit and equity markets (i.e. financial market liberalisation). But we contend that the biggest factor was the creation of new financial instruments.

A new form of liquidity (i.e. money) was being created outside the central bankers' control (Figure 7). And this 'liquidity' was in excess of the needs of the 'real economy' to create more GDP and instead pumped up asset prices.

Some would deny this as an explanation of rising asset values. What about the impact of increased labour productivity during the disinflation decades? Surely, that justifies higher asset values?

But much of the expansion in liquidity is not commensurate with the great boosts to productivity we are told about. Yes, labour got more productive under disinflation, but what about capital productivity?

One thing that beliws increasing capital productivity is the explosion in credit and financial assets if funds in relation to GDP. A decade ago, it took two to three units of new credit to fund one new unit of GDP. Now the figure is closer to five. If more credit is needed to produce the same amount of goods and services, it is hard to argue that capital has got more productive. The same holds when the focus switches from looking at capital transfers, such as securitised debt, to the 'real' economy.

When measuring capital expenditure in GDP, economists usually count only investment in equipment, buildings and factories (in some countries, software has recently been added). So GDP accounting, and therefore productivity measurement, ignores most investment that occurs in creating brand names and goodwill among customers, in training people, or in streamlining or structuring organisations to prosper in the globalised economy, and in shuffling assets (accounting and investment).

Excluding these sorts of investment expenditures in the definition of capital formation is anachronistic. It says if you can't kick it, it isn't an investment. But the rich countries of the world are now predominantly service economies. Much of their investments cannot be kicked. One recent study that tried to measure investment in intangibles that you can't kick found that the true level of investment in the US was 60-70% above the official figures.

Conventional GDP accounting treats most of these 'intangible' assets as either costs (leading to the understatement of both profits and assets), or as transfers (in which case, GDP accounting doesn't include them at all). But if you add in intangible investments, then the productivity of capital is much lower and partly explains why the growth of liquidity has outstripped that of GDP in the last 20 years.

All this 'intangible' investment occurs within the corporate sector. So old GDP accounting means that business expenses are being overstated and profit and capital formation are being understated by the amount of 'intangible' investment. But the result is that, by increasing the amount of assets relative to GDP, capital productivity is reduced. In sum, we may be using more capital than we think and getting less productivity than we account for by the usual measurements.

New forms of liquidity

But what are these new forms of liquidity that constitute the foundation of New Monetarism?

NEW MONETARISM AND DISINFLATION

In the good old days of the 1960s and 1970s, central bankers set the supply and price of money. They issued 'power money', then the banks borrowed it and lent it, keeping some in reserve. And the sum of the whole thing (power money and bank lending) was liquidity measured traditionally as 'broad money', which corresponded to all the credit created by the banking sector.

Sure, there was also securitised debt, but this was nearly all government borrowing, at least outside the US. For this was in the days when Germans couldn't have credit cards and Koreans couldn't get mortgages. There was virtually no securitised debt of these sorts of credits.

As disinflation multiplied the value of financial assets, central banks progressively lost control of money. Financial players, increasingly sure of cheap money, began to introduce new-fangled financial instruments that created liquidity independently of the central bank. So central bank power money became a smaller and smaller part of total credit (Figure 8).

All this new money didn't boost officially-measured inflation because globalisation and technology kept down the prices of most things we buy rather than invest in. This was particularly true for the prices of manufactured products that bore the brunt of the increased competition from globalisation.

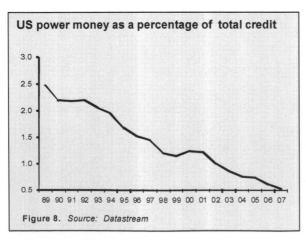

Figure 8. *Source: Datastream*

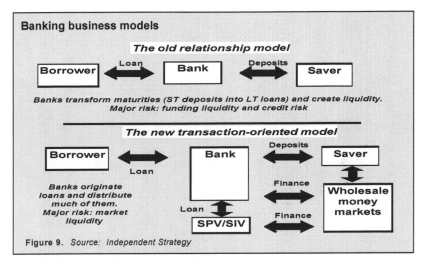

Figure 9. *Source: Independent Strategy*

In contrast, the price of assets began to soar, as money got cheaper and more plentiful. But no one counts asset price inflation as inflation. Indeed, asset price inflation is always called wealth creation until the credit bubble of underpriced capital that always lies at its base finally bursts.

New forms of securitised debt sprang up: mortgage debt, corporate debt and other asset-backed debt. This debt was really the old types of credit that were repackaged as bonds and sold onto other investors through financial markets. 'Origination and distribution' became banking's new business model (Figure 9).

These new forms of liquidity atomised risk, moving it off the balance sheets of the banks and into a myriad of new vehicles for 'structured finance' (see Figure 10 on page 10). By securitising loans into bonds and shifting it off balance sheets, banks were able to transfer risk to the investors in asset-backed securities (see Figure 11 on page 11).

NEW MONETARISM AND DISINFLATION

Banks' off-balance sheet conduits, SIV & SAC structure

The use of off-balance sheet conduits spread in the form of collateralised debt obligations (CDOs) and special investment vehicles (SIVs).

These structures housed all the new forms of securitised debt called asset-backed securities (ABS) and in particular, residential mortgage-backed securities (RMBS). These RMBS were a key ingredient of the CDO boom.

A CDO structure contained ABS purchases on the asset side and then spreads the credit risk by selling on the liabilities side different quality tranches of the debt through commercial paper. The SIV was a permanently capitalised structure managed by bank that holds CDOs and even more exotic instruments like collateralised synthetic obligations (CSOs) and collateralised loan obligations (CLOs), which invest in asset-backed commercial paper and swaps or leveraged bank loans.

By 2007, securitised debt products had reached $11trn globally, with more than half of it in the form of RMBS. In this way, the huge credit markets of residential and commercial mortgages, loans, credit cards and other consumer debt, that had previously been at the risk of banks and mortgage lenders, were now dispersed into a myriad of financial institutions.

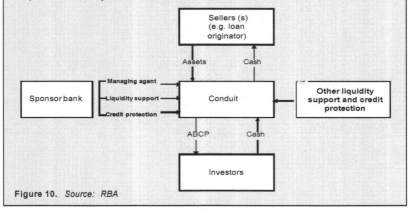

Figure 10. *Source: RBA*

Banks could now originate more credit and fund more risk assets. In effect, the banks were able to move the risk of lending onto the owners of these new forms of debt and thus expand their balance sheets.

New Monetarism was empowered: risk was atomised as loans and debt were moved off the balance sheets of depository institutions. Banks could now own more risk assets for less deposits; balance sheets could expand and lending capacity could rise.

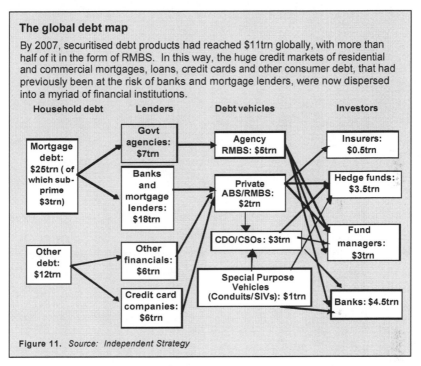

The global debt map

By 2007, securitised debt products had reached $11trn globally, with more than half of it in the form of RMBS. In this way, the huge credit markets of residential and commercial mortgages, loans, credit cards and other consumer debt, that had previously been at the risk of banks and mortgage lenders, were now dispersed into a myriad of financial institutions.

Figure 11. *Source: Independent Strategy*

Risk was diversified among more investors, but risk also rose because the final investor had much less information about the borrower. Moreover, it became increasingly unclear who was finally responsible for meeting the terms of the credit.

Positive feedback increased the risk: more lending created bullish investment led to flying asset prices, which in turn stimulated more bullishness and more leverage. The financial economy grew sharply relative to the real.

Derivatives: a hedge against risk or a credit Titanic?

The most important new form of liquidity was through the development of derivatives.

Are derivatives merely a form of 'neutral' transactional capital that increases the depth of financial markets without adding to risk or influencing asset prices? Or do they raise the risk of financial instability and collapse? The answer will help decide whether derivatives are for good or evil in our modern financial world.

The answer, of course, is both. Derivatives are not only transactional capital, but also a form of liquidity that influences asset prices. Metaphorically, derivatives are to financial liquidity what tilting the basin is to water — they increase the sloshing in whatever direction the market is leaning: bullish or bearish.

In a long-running bull market, derivatives create multiple means for more players to invest in more assets in a more leveraged fashion. This increases the 'investment power' (asset purchasing power) of money. It is pretty obvious that if one can buy a security that represents 100% of the value of an asset for 3-5% of the value of the asset, then an awful lot of liquidity has been freed up in relation to the underlying assets.

So, in their simplest form, many derivatives allow an investor to participate in 100% of the change in income or price of an underling asset for a fraction of its cost.

A nice image is that of a real estate derivative where an investor can buy or sell any change in the future value or rent of a shop or house at a fraction of its cost provided he accepts the greater risk of the derivative instrument. This increases market liquidity because buying the derivative is cheaper than buying the house. So it brings in new investors.

Unless demand for property has negative price elasticity the cheaper alternative — the derivative — will attract new players to the property market. That is how liquidity is created.

Derivative contracts are mainly based on bets on interest rates (Figure 12), although there has been a sharp increase in more exotic derivative instruments in recent years, which provide hedges in insurance, foreign exchange, equities, credit defaults, real estate, commodities, the weather and a wide range of other assets and risks..

Most derivatives are linked to assets in the US and Europe not in Asia (Figure 13). This is not a coincidence, but because the US and Europe are the places in the world with the fastest rising asset prices as a result of disinflation. This is where the most 'asset pricing money' was created.

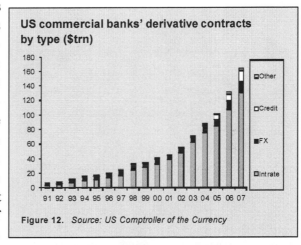

Figure 12. *Source: US Comptroller of the Currency*

In contrast, after the bursting of the Japanese stock bubble in 1989 and the Asian currency crises of 1997-8, financial institu-

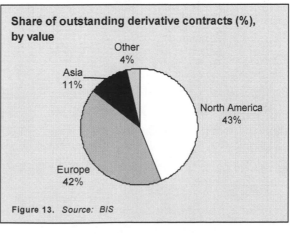

Figure 13. *Source: BIS*

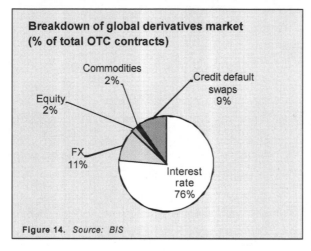

Breakdown of global derivatives market (% of total OTC contracts)

Commodities 2%

Credit default swaps 9%

Equity 2%

FX 11%

Interest rate 76%

Figure 14. *Source: BIS*

tions in Asia were preoccupied with the need to shrink their balance sheets, rather than pump them up using derivatives to do so.

As the vast majority of derivatives concern interest rates (e.g. swaps) or credit defaults (e.g. CDS), they are mostly used to transfer interest rate or default risks of a loan or bond off a bank's balance sheet to others like specialised hedge funds or insurance companies (Figure 14).

Interest-rate swaps can be used to fix the return or cost of an asset or liability by transferring the interest rate risk to another party. Thus, as in the case of securitised debt, derivatives free up credit capacity by spreading risk.

By spreading risk and increasing the shock absorption capacity of markets, derivatives can contribute to reducing the volatility of financial assets, along with many macroeconomic variables such as growth in GDP, wages, profits and inflation.

This creates widespread confidence that a low volatility world, characterised by contained inflation, low interest rates and a fairly flat, predictable and manageable economic cycle, will become a durable feature of the future. It is understandable that investors will want to take on more leverage than would otherwise be the case. This too generates liquidity. It is also why the notional value of derivatives dwarfs the underlying assets they represent.

In sum, derivatives do two things. They generate liquidity, much like securitised debt. And they provide insurance, principally against shifts in interest rates and credit default, but also for changes in a wide range of other asset prices, such as real estate, commodities, energy and foreign exchange.

The insurance function dominates the liquidity one. Derivatives improve the structure of the watertight bulkheads on the good ship of finance. So, if an iceberg of financial crisis should puncture one compartment, it won't sink the financial ship.

There is some evidence for this. In the very recent past, bubbles have burst without causing a generalised financial market crash — US equities in 2000, bankruptcies like Refco and LTCM, Aussie and UK housing in 2004, US housing and a bucket of Middle-Eastern equity markets in 2006).

No wonder bank regulators took the view that derivatives are basically good news. So they allowed the banks to create more loans to replace those for which derivatives have taken the risk off the balance sheet, although the banks must continue to provide for counterparty risk. This added to credit growth. In other words, the regulators believed that, although derivatives make the vessel of liquidity bigger, they made it safer and less volatile.

As a result, in the US, the value of derivative contracts held by the five major US banks were allowed to rise to 350% of their risk capital and nearly 100% of capital for the top 25 US banks (Figure 15).

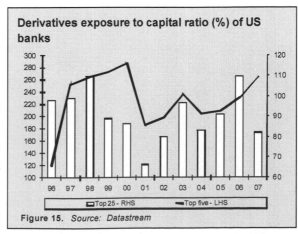

Figure 15. *Source: Datastream*

However, it is our contention that the bank regulators were ignoring the 'evil' side of the derivatives explosion. For if derivatives were a form of underpriced liquidity that created asset bubbles, then the impact of any bursting of these credit bubbles would become magnified by the size of any losses in the derivative markets.

This is where the story gets darker.

CHAPTER TWO

Derivatives and risk

CDX: defining the risk

Derivatives are a form of insurance. Therefore, the losses by a party that sells insurance are the gains of the buyer of insurance. It should net out to zero. So how could derivatives endanger the stability of the financial system and make New Monetarism a destructive force? The answer is when the losses are so large that the underwriter of them can't pay. How could this happen, where would the burden of unpaid losses fall and with what consequences?

A good start to find out is to look at the credit insurance market or CDX. Credit insurance is kernel to the behaviour of the liquidity pyramid under New Monetarism. Key among its functions are shifting credit risk off the balance sheets of deposit-taking institutions, allowing them to expand credit more than if the risk were maintained on their balance sheets;

Also, credit insurance improves the credit ratings and access to financial markets of entities with weak fundamentals, by allowing them to assume the ratings of counterparties that guarantee their debt;

Insurance allows lending institutions to manage their exposure to credit cycle risks, while broadening liquidity by spreading ownership of risk to non-bank financial intermediaries.

Outstanding global CDS can be measured by the notional value of contracts. The notional value of a CDS is its face value used to calculate payments. The face value of each CDS is representative of the par value of the insured credit. Because there are many more CDS contracts than the credit they insure, the notional value of issued CDS is normally a multiple of the underlying credit (loans or bonds).

DERIVATIVES AND RISK

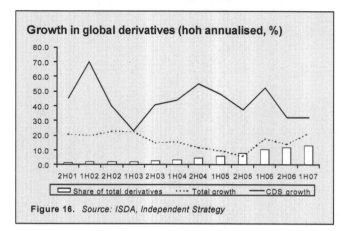

Growth in global derivatives (hoh annualised, %)

Figure 16. *Source: ISDA, Independent Strategy*

According to the International Swaps and Derivatives Association (ISDA) and the Bank for International Settlements (BIS), over-the counter (OTC) credit default swaps have been the fastest-growing derivatives over the last five years (Figure 16). They reached a notional value of $45trn by June 2007. But, as a proportion of total derivatives, CDS are still less than 10-12%, with over 70% of derivatives contracts in interest-rate swaps.

When defining risk from derivatives, notional value is misleading. Interest-rate derivatives, though measured by their notional value, only create a liability or asset equal to the difference between the swapped interest rate (when the derivative was transacted) and today's interest rate on the same underlying debt instrument. In other words, no one 'owes' the underlying (notional) value — only the interest-spread between the actual and contracted rate.

Similarly, in CDS markets every insurer or seller of a part of the risk of an underlying credit counts the total notional value of that credit as a transaction. So if ten investors split the default risk of a $100 credit among them, then the notional amount of the CDS outstanding will rise to $1000 ($100 times 10).

Nevertheless, for a CDS, someone somewhere is on the line to pay the full notional value of the underlying bond/credit if the issuer defaults. So comparing the value of CDS contracts with interest-rate derivatives to gauge risk underestimates the significant capital exposure from CDS contracts.

Indeed, what worries some investors is that this 'tiny' amount of CDS may blow up the whole system, just like collateralised debt obligations (CDOs) nearly did. CDOs are just a tiny fraction of credit derivatives, which are in turn just a small part of the notional value of all derivatives. In derivative markets what appears small and insignificant can nevertheless be lethal!

So how big is the risk from CDS? The traditional way of trying to measure the risk of derivatives to the financial system uses market values as its basic building bloc. The market value of CDS exposure can be measured in different ways, eventually reducing it to the current credit exposure (Figure 17).

The market value of credit default swaps

The gross market value of a derivative contract is computed as the absolute value of the open contract, with either positive or negative replacement value, evaluated at market prices. The positive and negative values are added together (i.e. the minus is ignored in the case of negative values). Values are not 'netted' for bilateral agreements or collateral (more on this later). Thus the gross market value is the cost of replacing all open contracts at market prices and provides a measure of derivatives market risk as well as of their economic significance that is comparable across the different categories of derivative products.

Gross market value can be split into gross positive fair value for contracts that show a profit, which the bank is 'owed' by its counterparties; and gross negative fair value, where the bank owes money to its counterparties — both measures being calculated without netting. Gross positive fair value is the amount the bank would lose if all of its counterparties defaulted without netting. Gross negative fair value is the loss the bank's counterparties would suffer if the bank failed and there were no netting contracts or collateral.

Current credit exposure is the positive value amount of derivative contracts that the bank would receive (and is therefore at risk of losing if there is counterparty failure) if all existing derivative contract(s) were liquidated today. The positive market value of contracts is thus reduced ('netted') by legally enforceable bilateral netting agreements. The sum of the bank's derivatives with negative market values (money owed by the bank were they to settle today) are called current credit liabilities and are also computed after netting. However, current credit liabilities are not counted in current credit exposure because they will be captured in some other entity's current credit exposure as positive values.

Figure 17. Source: BIS, Independent Strategy

DERIVATIVES AND RISK

The CDS chain and delta hedging

Let's work an example of CDS netting.

Bank A wants to buy protection on 80% of a credit of E100 it made to the Slime Corporation. Bank A buys a CDS from Bank B for E80 to do this. Now Bank B is on the hook for 80% of the E100 credit that Bank A made to the Slime Corp if it defaults on the credit. Bank B won't want to retain all of that risk on its balance sheet. So Bank B buys a CDS from Bank C for 50% or E40 of its CDS exposure to Bank A.

Bank A's credit exposure is now E20 (E100 less the bought CDS of E80); Bank B's credit exposure is E40 (the CDS it sold to Bank A = E80 less the CDS it bought from Bank C= E40)... and so on. This we call the CDS chain.

Delta measures the change in the price of a derivative instrument to changes in the value of the underlying asset (upon which it is 'derived').

Delta hedging can be achieved by buying or selling an amount of the underlying asset that corresponds to the delta of the portfolio. By adjusting the amount bought or sold on new positions, the portfolio delta can be made to sum to zero and the portfolio is then 'delta neutral'.

A portfolio that is delta neutral is effectively hedged such that its overall value will not change for small changes in the price of its underlying instrument.

In order make things more understandable, we have simplified hedging in this report by assuming that the relationship between the values of the CDS and the underlying credit is linear when it is usually convex. This allows us to use a constant delta hedged proportion throughout the CDS chain.

Figure 18. *Source: Independent Strategy*

To measure the current credit exposure, the essence of risk control is <u>netting.</u> Netting means deducting losses from gains on contracts with the same counterparty, or deducting legally enforceable bilateral netting' contracts within the same risk category (e.g. being long and short the same risk).

Netting can also include the deduction of collateral held by the bank against derivative contracts. In calculating the current credit exposure of an intermediary's CDS contracts, netting deducts the amount of credit risk the CDS seller (the provider of credit insurance) has laid off by buying CDS (purchasing credit insurance) from other parties.

This is <u>delta hedging</u>. Delta hedging is defined as controlling the risk of a derivative or asset position by buying or selling derivative instruments or their underlying assets with opposite values. We call the proportion of risk laid off in this way the <u>delta hedged proportion</u> (Figure 18).

CDS: market losses

What's been described so far is a series of market-based risk measures that constitute a perfectly reasonable way of judging the market risk of all parties at any given time. What it yields is very reassuring.

In Q2'07, according to the BIS, financial institutions held OTC derivatives of all types with a notional value of $516trn globally, but with a gross market value of 'only' $11trn and an estimated gross credit exposure (after deducting from gross market value legally enforceable bilateral netting arrangements) of about one-quarter of that gross market value ($2.7trn) — see Figure 17 for definitions.

In other words, using this method of measuring risk, only 0.5% of the notional value of derivatives ends up as the gross credit exposure of the financial system, although that is still equivalent to around 5% of global GDP (Figure 19).

Nevertheless, as the credit cycle tightens and the global economy slows, corporate defaults will increase and credit quality will deteriorate. As a result, the cost of credit insurance will rise and sellers of protection will lose money on their CDS contracts. That should mean that net sellers of protection would take the hit.

In 2006, banks globally were net buyers of protection ($304bn) and credit guarantors (monolines)

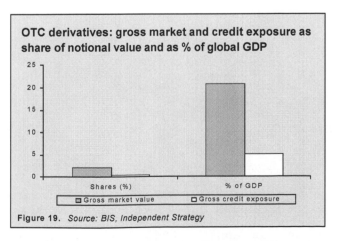

Figure 19. Source: BIS, Independent Strategy

and other insurance companies were net <u>sellers</u> of protection ($355bn and $395bn respectively). (The buying and selling of credit protection does not add up to zero because net buyers of protection, such as hedge funds and pension funds, are poorly covered statistically.) So, as defaults rise, the banks should stand to gain and the guarantors and insurance companies to lose.

But things are not so simple! The net protection bought by the banks and other financial intermediaries from insurance and financial guaranty companies is the residual of massive stocks of credit derivatives (around $24.6trn gross bought positions) on banks' and broker dealers' books. These stocks include single name CDS (about 40%); index products (45%); as well as CDOs and portfolio products (e.g. CDS on asset-backed securities).

That means the market risk is not well expressed by the net balance of bought and sold protection. It is more a function of the credit quality of the CDS 'book' and also how the 'stock' is traded. The value of this CDS stock can be severely impaired by problems within a category of debt (e.g. asset-backed securities) or even in a major single name (e.g. GM). That's particularly so because CDS trading is highly concentrated in just a few names (the top 20 names account for 34% of the business, according to Fitch). So the credit base of the CDS market is poorly diversified.

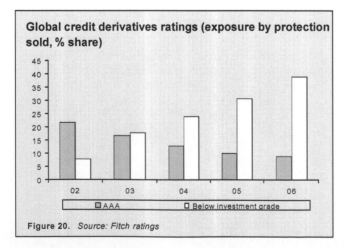

Global credit derivatives ratings (exposure by protection sold, % share)

□ AAA   □ Below investment grade

Figure 20. *Source: Fitch ratings*

The quality of the underlying credits is another problem (Figure 20). The credit quality of the bonds insured by CDS has deteriorated dramatically and continuously, reflecting the scramble for yield in the days of the liquidity bubble, with speculative and unrated issues accounting for 40% of total stock of gross protection sold at the end of 2006 compared to 8% in 2002. There has been a matching decline in top-quality credits insured as a proportion of the gross protection sold from 22% in 2002 to 9% in 2006.

Moreover, many banks have moved towards becoming net sellers of protection pretty dramatically in recent years, even if overall the sector remains a net buyer. Fitch reckons 45% of the 44 banks surveyed are now net sellers. Indeed, Germany (uniquely) has a banking sector that is a net seller of protection ($76bn at end-2006). In general, banks have become active investors in CDS rather than using them to offset the risk of their loan books. That is a shift from a low to a high-risk activity.

We shall really only find out where the big losses are after they become apparent. But, given the nature of credit derivatives (that every bought protection is a liability for someone else), the risks are already out there and the losses will happen.

Our estimate of such market price losses is crude in the extreme. We can look at what happened to CDS values in 1989-90 and 2001 and apply that loss ratio to the much larger outstanding value of CDS credit insurance today. That yields an estimated market loss of $10-40bn.

CDX defaults

There is a weakness in the market pricing method of assessing losses from CDS. It depends on markets functioning normally. What we really want to test for are losses caused by default of the credits underlying CDS and the risk of counterparty default in the CDS chains created by delta hedging.

DERIVATIVES AND RISK

This requires a different approach to risk. Surprisingly, although the notional value of CDS will often exceed that of the insured credit many times over, total CDS losses on a defaulted credit will equal and not exceed the loss on the insured credit (unless there is a counterparty default in the CDS chain).

Measured in notional values, the ratio of CDS to the par value of the insured credit is a function of the delta hedged proportion*. But the value of this ratio does not affect losses to the holders of CDS and only changes the aggregate notional value (Figure 21).

This enables us to do some back-of-the-envelope stress-testing in the real world. According to the BIS in its latest Triennial Survey, there were about $51trn of credit derivatives outstanding at end-June 2007. About 88% of these were CDS. Thus the notional value of CDS was $45trn.

In general, lending intermediaries such as banks do not want to retain more than 5-15% of the credit risk of any single credit on their own balance sheets. So the delta hedged proportion is 0.85-0.95. In other words, 85-95% of the credit risk is sold onto another player by buying a CDS. For the sake of simplicity, we use a delta hedged proportion of 90% (or 0.90) and we assume this is linear.

That means that the BIS's notional value $45trn for outstanding CDS represents 'real' underlying credits of $5trn. That's a princely sum, being equal to 20% of the combined risk assets of US and European banks and more than double their tier-one capital! But to be as scary as it looks, it must go bust and be lost (after allowing for asset recovery).

The arithmetic of CDXS contracts: the tree and the sawmills

The arithmetic of CDS lends itself to hyperbole, but the reality is often more mundane. The number of CDX contracts per unit of insured debt is determined by the delta hedged proportion. If the delta hedged proportion is 90% (90% of each party's risk on a credit is offset by buying protection for that amount), there will be a chain of CDS contracts for each bond, resulting in CDS contracts with notional values as high as ten times the par value of the underlying credit (assuming linear delta hedging). So, if the value of the underlying credit falls by 10, the losses in the CDS market will be 10 times as large because there are 10 times more CDS contracts than there are bonds — right? No — this is very often the basis for some scary statements about the potential for CDS losses, but it is wrong.

Think of the insured credit as a tree and every CDS contract as a sawmill. In our example, there is one tree and 10 sawmills. Each sawmill chops off one-tenth of the original volume. But the tree remains a tree. So each of the ten sawmills has counted one tree as processed. That makes ten trees. Sawing off a bit of the tree reduces its volume or insured risk. Each time the same tree is sawn up, it is counted as an additional tree. In a CDS chain, each contract is counted as the par value of the insured credit. But each sawmill reduces the volume of the trunk (the risk) by one-tenth of the original volume. At the end of the chain of sawmills (or contracts) all of the chopped-off bits (of trunk or risk) add up to 100% of the volume (risk) of the tree. The credit, like the tree, has been counted ten times.

So, when the value of the credit or the tree falls by say 10%, the value of all the trees counted (the 10 notional values) all fall and the loss looks huge. But the real loss is only 10% of the original tree (or credit). In reality, if no party in the CDS chain defaults, the CDS losses on protection sold will exactly equal the losses on the underlying credit — no more and no less.

That's because the multiple CDS contracts spread the same credit risk as the underlying credit among many more players, but in progressively smaller slices that add up to the same risk as the credit itself. And the CDS contracts are evenly split between those selling and those buying insurance. Only the sellers of insurance make a loss if the price of the underlying credit deteriorates.

As long as the CDS chain is without default, any decline in the value of the credit insured will result in a decline in the total notional value of CDS contracts many times greater than itself. But this does not represent the loss born by sellers of credit insurance, which will be equal to the loss on the bond.

All of this changes dramatically if there is a counterparty default in the CDS chain. This will cause other CDS chains to collapse if they pass through the failed entity. And, because CDS chains involve very few players, systemic risks rises exponentially with any counterparty failure. In a default, any losses on insured securities are compounded by unsettled fees for protection sold and by uncollect-able amounts of protection bought from a failed entity.

Theoretically a CDS contract for protection only pays out the insured par value of the underlying credit if the original bond can be delivered. But, as there are far more CDS contracts than bonds, this can be a problem that can lift the price of defaulted bonds beyond their economic worth. Non-standard procedures for settling CDS of defaulted credits have resulted in long delays and expensive legal procedures to get settlements. Consequently, moves are afoot by major banks to set up a central clearing house to settle contracts.

Figure 21. *Source: Independent Strategy*

How likely is this and to what degree? Looking back at corporate defaults for the period for which statistics exist, we find that the maximum rate of corporate defaults was about 3% in the 1990s recession (Figure 22). However, corporate speculative grade bond defaults run as high as 10% (in 1990-91 and again in 2001) according to Moody's* (Figure 23).

Using a weighted default ratio of 5% (3% for investment grade and 10% for sub-investment grade), which is close to what Moody's is forecasting this year, would mean that credits (with outstanding CDS) with a par value of $250bn would default.

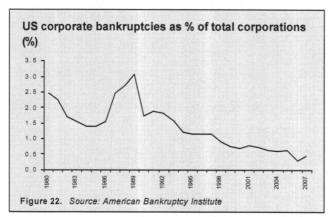

US corporate bankruptcies as % of total corporations (%)

Figure 22. *Source: American Bankruptcy Institute*

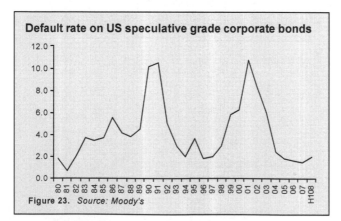

Default rate on US speculative grade corporate bonds

Figure 23. *Source: Moody's*

Assuming an asset recovery ratio of 30% (the same range as we use for sub-prime mortgages, but very low for AA to BBB-type corporate credit), the hit to financial sector would be $175bn. That compares to $1900bn in tier-one capital of the combined European and US financial systems, where most of these losses would occur.

Now that is a sizeable hit and it would cause further substantial global credit contraction of 0.5-1.0%. Add in the market losses on non-defaulted CDS, as well as losses on downgraded bonds as a result of monoline woes throughout the CDS chain and we reach our forecast for the shrinkage of bank credit in the EU and US of 8-9%.

CDS: counterparty risk

But all of that would pale into insignificance if a major counterparty in a CDS chain went bust (see Figure 21 on page 25). What could cause this to happen?

When it comes to counterparty risk, the core issue to consider is the concentration of ownership of CDS risk. The smaller the number of players, the greater is the risk that netting is a sham, a sort of musical chairs game that disintegrates when the music stops.

According to Fitch, the top ten institutions represented 62% of all credit insurance exposure (i.e. aggregate balance sheet values of credit bought and sold) and 89% of the total notional amount of credit insurance bought and sold in 2006 (Figure 24).

If delta hedging is carried out by repetitive transactions among only a few players, then risk diversification may be an illusion. Indeed delta hedging, by gen-

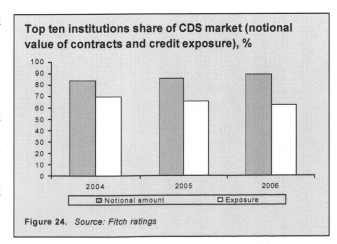

Top ten institutions share of CDS market (notional value of contracts and credit exposure), %

Figure 24. *Source: Fitch ratings*

erating a false sense of confidence, may actually increase counterparty risk.

In a CDS market dominated by just a few players, everyone ends up holding everyone else's credit. At some point, the knock-on risk of failure anywhere in a small system becomes apparent to all. There is no real risk diversification — so if one party fails, they take everyone else down in the chain.

Ten to fifteen players might be enough to ensure proper diversification of risk in a stable credit environment with little risk of systemic failure. But this would not be the case in an unstable environment. In a market with few participants, where linked counterparty risk is very obvious, all participants will pull back when instability occurs because they can see the knock-on consequences of counterparty failure anywhere in the system. This will cause a dramatic shrinkage of CDS volumes.

The banks are unlikely to be where to look for a counterparty default. They will have to shrink their balance sheets and go through the painful process of inflicting deleveraging on their clients. But they are strong enough to withstand the hit. So should the story end there?

Well, it doesn't because of the risk inherent in other sectors. First, the impact of counterparty failure on liquidity may be worse if it affects non-bank financial intermediaries, like hedge funds, as these have less of a capital cushion to withstand the shock.

Hedge funds (though small players in CDS in comparison to the banks) account for up to 60% of CDS index trading, according to Greenwich. Fitch reckons that 40% of CDS contracts are for sub-investment grade entities and that "hedge funds may be an important source of protection selling for below investment-grade credits".

Fluctuations in balance sheets of non-bank financial intermediaries (including hedge funds and prime brokers) are naturally highly pro-cyclical in normal cycles. In an abnormal cycle, driven by counterparty default, balance sheet contraction in this sector, vital as it is as a generator of market liquidity, could then bring financial markets to the edge of a cliff.

CHAPTER THREE

The Liquidity Pyramid

Our measurement of liquidity is not that of an economist. It encompasses variables that provide evidence of risk appetite, credit multipliers and the quantity of money and sums them all into a Liquidity Pyramid. The pyramid is a symbol and expression of the supply and demand for liquidity.

We define liquidity as *any form of money that can be used to buy goods or services, or invest in an asset, to freeze the cost or return of holding an asset or liability, or to transfer ownership or risks of ownership to another party.* What this definiton does is to expand the traditional measure of liquidity as broad money or total bank credit so that the new definition encompasses all forms of credit. It does this by adding to the old definition all forms of securitised debt as well as debt that is synthetically securitised by having its interest-rate and default risk removed from the banks' balance sheets using derivatives.

Today global liquidity is like a massive pyramid standing on its head (Figure 25). It represents nearly twelve years of GDP and until the onset of the credit crunch was growing at least five times faster than GDP.

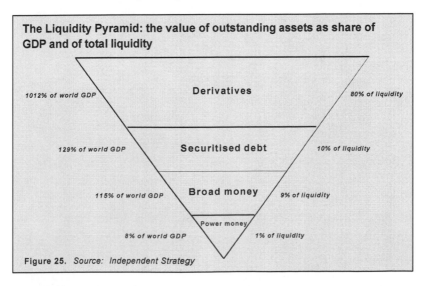

The Liquidity Pyramid: the value of outstanding assets as share of GDP and of total liquidity

Derivatives — 1012% of world GDP — 80% of liquidity

Securitised debt — 129% of world GDP — 10% of liquidity

Broad money — 115% of world GDP — 9% of liquidity

Power money — 8% of world GDP — 1% of liquidity

Figure 25. *Source: Independent Strategy*

THE LIQUIDITY PYRAMID

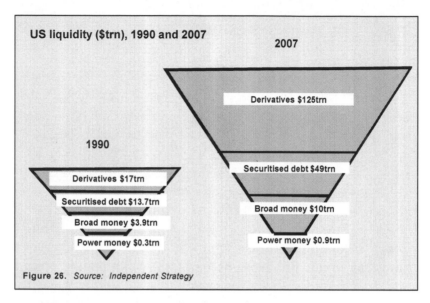

US liquidity ($trn), 1990 and 2007

2007

Derivatives $125trn

1990

Securitised debt $49trn

Derivatives $17trn

Securitised debt $13.7trn

Broad money $10trn

Broad money $3.9trn

Power money $0.3trn

Power money $0.9trn

Figure 26. *Source: Independent Strategy*

Traditional money and new liquidity to GDP (indexed 1992=100)

☐ Derivatives

☐ Debt

■ Money aggregates

Figure 27. *Source: US Comptroller of the Currency, Datastream, Independent Strategy*

The biggest, fastest growing slug of liquidity (derivatives) is destined for financial assets, not shopping for things and services. No wonder the price of the former soared and the price of the latter disinflated!

The liquidity pyramid grew like wildfire. Between 1990 and 2005 in the US, it expanded by 300% while GDP grew only 80% (Figure 26).

Securitised debt alone grew by a factor by 200%. So the liquidity to buy financial assets grew twice as fast as the money to shop (Figure 27).

Excess liquidity growth over and above nominal GDP growth has been much faster than central bankers dare admit. But the compartmentalisation of this liquidity has stopped it generating price inflation of goods and services.

As important as the composition of the liquidity pyramid in terms of financial instruments is the changing composition of institutions that lend and borrow using them. Hedge fund and broker balance sheets are around half the size of the commercial banks in the US and one-quarter in Europe (Figure 28). Hedge funds and their creditor counterparties, chiefly prime brokers, dealers and investment banks, are included in our liquidity pyramid under non-depository financial institutions (NDFI). In recent decades, the NDFI sector's balance sheet, a measure of the credit and liquidity it creates, has mushroomed from a tenth to around 40% of the value of bank balance sheets in the US (Figure 29).

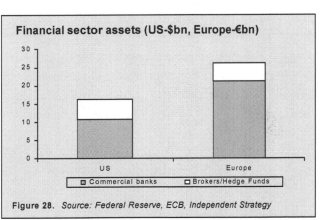

Figure 28. *Source: Federal Reserve, ECB, Independent Strategy*

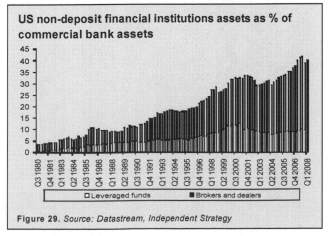

Figure 29. *Source: Datastream, Independent Strategy*

THE LIQUIDITY PYRAMID

NDFI liquidity is exclusively asset money and this has a direct impact on financial asset prices. The balance sheets of banks have also become more pro-cyclical and volatile as their assets and liabilities were increasingly 'marketised'.

But commercial bank balance sheets are still less volatile than NDFI ones because banks create credit for many other purposes other than financial market investment. So the balance sheets of NDFIs are highly geared to asset price cycles. They act in a pro-cyclical manner, reinforcing bull and bear market phases and through them economic cycles.

The reason for this is that NDFIs manage their balance sheets so as to maintain a constant ratio of leverage to total assets*. Both assets and liabilities of NDFIs are dominated by repos, meaning that NDFIs lend and borrow based upon collateral of assets that are constantly marked to market. As asset prices fluctuate, leverage must constantly be adjusted (Figure 30).

In a bear market, as asset prices fall, leverage is reduced. This causes lenders to ask for more collateral on existing loans and borrowers to sell assets so as to reduce the need for such loans and for additional collateral.

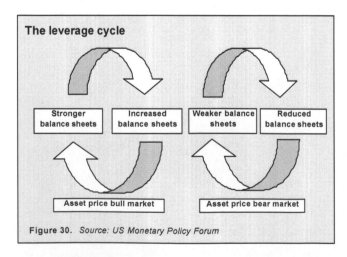

Figure 30. *Source: US Monetary Policy Forum*

The opposite happens in a bull market when rising asset prices cause the balance sheets of NDFIs to expand. The liquidity this creates is used to in-

34

vest in assets, boosting their prices and creating demand and collateral for more borrowing to make more investments.

How underpriced capital became the US's most successful export

What is good for the US is good for the globe. The US 'invented' New Monetarism and liquidity pyramid came of age there. However, today in Europe, the duplication of the US liquidity pyramid is almost complete. But the way in which the US transmits its model to the world is not limited to other countries emulating its monetary architecture. There are two other transmission mechanisms that make New Monetarism, or rather the liquidity it generates, the US's most successful export.

One is that, as 'wealth' is created, it boosts consumption. Part of the additional 'wealth' is turned into shopping money (through selling assets, home equity withdrawals or other forms of increased borrowing). Rising asset values also mean that consumers save less from their incomes because their assets do their saving for them simply by increasing in value. As they get richer, consumers feel more confident and shopping is fun.

This is true everywhere. But in the case of the US, excessive consumer expenditure means that the country spends more than it produces and this creates a current account deficit equal to its savings shortfall (Figure 31).

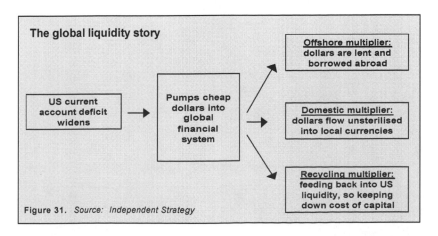

Figure 31. *Source: Independent Strategy*

THE LIQUIDITY PYRAMID

Thus a US current account deficit means that dollars created by the liquidity pyramid, which get spent on excess consumption, get sent abroad to pay for imports and are left in the hands of foreigners. Some of those dollars never return home and end up in foreign monetary systems and in offshore banks. There they may be lent and borrowed many times over so that each dollar can get multiplied into many.

Some dollars get changed into local currency in countries running an external surplus with the US. Those dollars, converted into local currency, are deposited in local banks. If the local currency equivalent of the dollar inflow is not borrowed by the central bank (i.e. sterilised), once again the credit multiplier goes to work.

Those dollars that are changed into local currency end up in the central bank. The central bank (or finance ministry in some Asian countries) recycles them back to the US. There they are invested in fixed income securities, so sustaining or adding to, the US credit pyramid.

At the end of the day — or, more precisely, when the global credit multiplier is done — one little dollar repeats the miracle of the loaves and fishes.

The story of how the US influences global liquidity doesn't stop there. In recent years, wealth creation and expanding consumption made the US the fastest-growing economy in the world. As a result, Fed policy became global monetary policy to a significant extent.

Because other major economies (Japan and Europe) were much weaker than the US, they couldn't afford to let their currencies strengthen against the dollar. To do so would have damaged their exports and boosted their imports, hitting their own output and jobs.

So, they had to operate a closet dollar-peg currency system, keeping their currencies in line with the US on foreign exchanges. The only way to do that was to keep their currencies cheap and mirror low US interest rates.

The rest followed. Cheap money allowed many of their financial markets to run riot, creating the liquidity pyramid that inflated asset prices just as in the US.

Japan: the alternative global ATM: free cash on demand

It would be wrong to attribute all growth in international liquidity to the US. Nor is a *current account* deficit the only way to generate global liquidity. Japan was a big contributor to global liquidity through its *capital* account deficit. Capital has been abnormally cheap priced in Japan. But in Japan's case this is to combat deflation and facilitate restructuring, particularly in the banking sector. This encouraged Japanese investors to pour funds into higher-yielding assets abroad. At one point, Japanese housewives owned nearly half of New Zealand's bond market!

Non-Japanese investors also borrowed cheap yen to buy higher-yielding foreign assets too (Figure 32). This operation is called the Great Carry Trade (Figure 33 on page 39). As borrowed yen are sold to purchase the currency of the higher -yielding asset before investing in it, the yen became the most undervalued major currency in the world (Figure 34).

The carry trade

Everyone in Japan benefited from a weak yen. The major short yen players onshore in Japan were households and Japanese banks. Households (through investment trusts) quintupled their exposure to high-

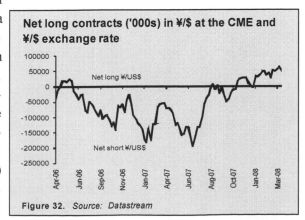

Net long contracts ('000s) in ¥/$ at the CME and ¥/$ exchange rate

Net long ¥/US$

Net short ¥/US$

100000
50000
0
-50000
-100000
-150000
-200000
-250000

Apr-06 Jun-06 Sep-06 Nov-06 Jan-07 Apr-07 Jun-07 Aug-07 Oct-07 Jan-08 Mar-08

Figure 32. *Source: Datastream*

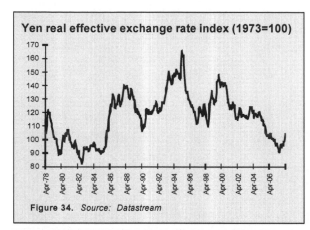

Yen real effective exchange rate index (1973=100)

Figure 34. *Source: Datastream*

yielding foreign assets, though they were still less than 3% of household financial assets. Also, household foreign investment exposure is counted in yen. The yen has been very weak. So part of the build-up in Japanese household assets was not a flow but simply a currency revaluation effect.

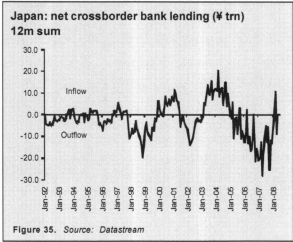

Japan: net crossborder bank lending (¥ trn) 12m sum

Inflow

Outflow

Figure 35. *Source: Datastream*

Japan's balance of payments tells just part of the story. Japan runs a large current account surplus. FDI outflows are much smaller, if growing. Yet its international reserves virtually stopped rising. So capital was being recycled abroad by households and banks, not by little green men from Mars.

The Japanese financial institutions were lending heavily abroad (Figure 35). Outside the banks, Japanese investment institutions were all very, very long foreign assets.

Sources of yen carry trade

Chart A: Japan — investment trusts, foreign currency assets (¥trn)

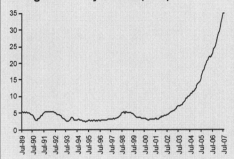

What are the sources of the yen carry trade and how big is it? The main sources include Japanese citizens who have conducted a form of the carry trade in seeking higher yield by investing in foreign assets. This is revealed in the increase in Japanese holdings of foreign assets held through investment trusts, which citizens have been able to buy through the post office since 2005. This comes to about ¥7trn annually, or $60bn, accumulating to ¥30trn by the end of 2005 (Chart A).

Chart B: Share of Japanese household financial assets in foreign-denominated investments (%)

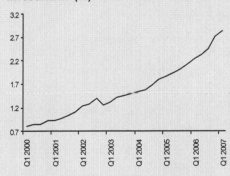

Each year households are switching about 0.4% pt of their financial assets into FX-denominated investments (Chart B). So this is a powerful structural force behind the carry trade.

A much bigger source of the yen carry trade is where Japanese banks borrow short in yen and lend long in FX (Chart C). This adds up to about $170bn annually. There are also indications that foreign banks borrow in yen to fund positions in higher-yielding currencies (worth about another $30bn). This is the big swing factor in flows out of Japan that affects the carry trade.

Chart C: Japan net crossborder banking flows, on a 12-mth sum (¥trn)

Also, contributing to the carry trade is hedging by foreign investors when buying Japanese equities or bonds (there is probably quite a lot of this as foreign net purchases of Japanese equities are strong and yet the yen is weak). As long as the yen looks weak, this hedging will continue. Overall, the yen carry trade could be around $300bn a year.

Figure 33. *Source: Datastream*

39

THE LIQUIDITY PYRAMID

The accepted wisdom is that, as long as yen interest rates and the volatility of foreign assets and their underlying currencies are low, the yen carry trade will continue.

But the correlation for the yen to the differential between Fed and BoJ policy rates is poor. There have been times when the yen has been very strong and the interest-rate differential for the US over Japan has stayed wide.

Moreover, the recent burst of yen weakness was unaccompanied by any increase in portfolio outflows. Indeed, those flows (including those of Japanese households) have actually reversed since the credit crunch began.

The reason is that much of the yen carry trade is purely speculative and not captured by Japan's payments data.

The yen carry trade is also the result of a process of creating 'synthetic yen' by offshore derivative markets. How does this work?

A mortgage borrower in a Baltic state (or Spain, Hungary or Austria) can opt for a "yen" mortgage. He or she receives the credit in local currency. But the borrower pays a yen interest rate (plus a generous spread for the local bank), not the higher local currency rate. The local bank then goes into the derivatives markets and shorts (borrows) the yen against the euro for an amount equal to the mortgage it just granted. The bank receives the difference between euro and yen rates because Japanese interest rates are lower than the local ones. This is called the yield pick-up on the carry trade (i.e. you get paid to borrow yen and invest in a higher-yielding currency or asset). Some of this interest-rate gain is passed onto the borrower and some of it the bank keeps to fatten its own margins.

The mortgage borrower assumes the asset price risk of a property, the currency risk and the interest-rate risk. The bank holds the counter-party risk on the yen trade and the risk that the borrower goes belly up. We have just witnessed the creation of synthetic yen using forex derivative markets to the value of the deposit the bank lent as a 'yen' mortgage.

None of this ever touched the shores of Japan or entered the Japanese BOP stats unless the counter-party to the yen trade was a Japanese bank! That means that most of the forces that drove the yen down were off-shore through the shorting of 'synthetic' yen in derivative markets.

The best fit for forecasting the yen was probably between the short yen positions on the Chicago Mercantile Exchange (and other forex markets) and the yen exchange rate. In other words, speculation drove the yen.

But here is the rub. Asset bubbles some times burst of their own volition and not because of a radical shift in fundamentals such as interest rates or economic data. Such collapses usually occur after speculative fervour and volumes reach extremes driven by 'thinning' stories and after the 'insiders' have exited the trade. That is what happend to the yen carry trade.

Those that thought the yen carry trade would go on making them money until Japanese interest rates closed the gap with the US were proven wrong. In the ultimate stage of a bubble's life, the market itself is the only determinant of reversal, not the external data.

A bigger risk to the yen trade was the volatility of the destination curren-cies (like the New Zealand dollar or Hungarian forint) or assets (housing, bonds) invested in. If their volatility rose, the reward/risk ratio of the carry trade would fall and money would exit and return to yen for safety or to repay lenders.

Once the direction of the yen changed since the credit crunch began, that is what happened. That is not to say that there will be a repeat of the fiasco when the hedge funds were forced to reverse positions in 1998. This time, households and banks are the bigger players and are likely to reverse more gradually. Nevertheless, the yen carry trade is over and some 13% of global liquidity will start to shrink (that's the amount generated in yen).

The damage done by a rising yen will not be confined to Japanese exporters. The profit margins of small and medium businesses (which supply the blue-chip exporters) and Japanese banks' and institutional investors' balance sheets (again!) will take a big hit.

There will be many other losers. Much other weeping is starting to be heard in far-flung corners of the earth. The noisiest will be in the small markets and economies that were the recipients of the long side of the short yen trade: the New Zealand dollar, Indian equities and EM debt — not to mention the big losers: the dollar and US treasuries. The holders of yen mortgages in Hungary, Spain and Austria are now feeling the pain. A falling tide lowers all boats!

CHAPTER FOUR

The Currency Accelerator

There's another character in our story of New Monetarism and its workings. There is a currency accelerator that modifies the traditional liquidity cycle by prolonging its expansionary phase. In so doing, it ensures that currency turmoil will be a factor in the collapse of liquidity-driven bubbles.

The synapse between global liquidity and the two of the world's major sources of it — the US and Japan — is not the only source of global liquidity outside domestic markets. There is another link. This is the Currency Accelerator (Figure 36).

At the top of the accelerator is world GDP, split by currency. Below this is the share of each of these currency blocs in world trade. The next layer down shows in what currency each bloc pays for its imports. The amounts of each currency used to pay for the imports ends up in an exporting country.

In the current account surplus countries, most foreign currency earned ends up in the central bank. Thus the final level or apex of the accelerator pyramid shows the breakdown by currency of central bank international reserves.

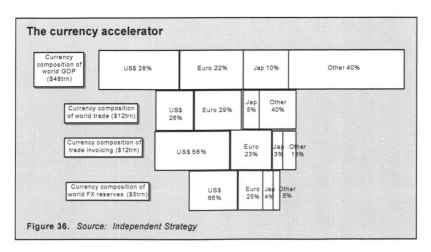

Figure 36. *Source: Independent Strategy*

THE CURRENCY ACCELERATOR

As currency flows from financing GDP to international trade and then to paying for imports, it becomes increasingly concentrated in dollar and euros and to a much lesser degree in yen.

At the level of GDP, the euro and the dollar account for 46% of the value of global currency value. The US and the eurozone account for 54% of the value of international trade, but for 83% of the currencies used to pay for it. Finally, the central banks of the current account surplus world receive and keep their international reserves even more in dollars and euros (91% of the total).

In effect, the 'real' economy of global GDP and international trade cascades like water over a series of narrowing weirs that increasingly focus transaction demand for currency to finance international trade in two or three of the world's greatest monies. Minor currencies of countries accounting for roughly half of global output and trade are filtered out in the process. To a degree, so is the yen. This is a contributory reason why the yen is a 'naturally' weak currency.

When the stream of concentrated currency reaches the portals of central banks — the point at which the water stops flowing and is stored in a reservoir — this domination of major currencies in international reserves is further concentrated by central bankers into the three major currencies that make up the liquidity pyramid.

The dominant role of the euro and dollar in international trade and central bank reserves prejudices their exchange rates towards the stronger side versus the yen and other currencies. It is also ensures that the major currencies in the global liquidity pyramid have enjoyed remarkably low volatility.

The exchange rate of currencies is set by a combination of transaction demand for global trade and asset demand for investment. The funnelling process of international trade favours the dollar and the euro versus the yen — and it favours the stability of all three versus the world's minor currencies. This is structural for as long as it lasts.

We have seen that the currency accelerator may contribute to yen weakness by focusing transaction demand for international trade on the dollar and the euro. The same may also be temporarily true of the liquidity pyramid.

While Japanese interest rates remain very low, yen are attractive to borrow and use to fund investment in other currencies' assets that yield more. Relatively little of this yen borrowing is hedged back into yen because this would deprive the carry trade of the return from a weakening borrowed currency and from low Japanese interest rates. And it would limit gains to those resulting from a change in the price of the asset invested in. The yen is thus borrowed and then sold into the currency of asset being invested in. So the yen is a short. That is why it has become structurally weak despite Japan's massive current account surplus.

Currency accelerator and liquidity bust

While the mechanisms of international trade are yen negative, those of the liquidity pyramid are only so for as long as yen is the major source of finance for the carry trade.

The 'real' economy progressively channels currency demand into the major currencies that drive global liquidity and central banks act to ensure that this pattern is preserved in the store of assets they control. Thus the global liquidity pyramid is being pumped by the mechanism of world trade.

Liquidity is boosted by global imbalances such as the US current account deficit and Japan's massive exports of savings, both of which can be traced to underpriced capital. But for the dollar, these weak fundamentals are suppressed by "real" economy demand for dollar as a medium of transaction in international trade and as the world's predominant reserve currency. This lends the dollar some stability, which in turn means that it can be used as the major currency in the liquidity pyramid. That generates further dollar demand and, in turn, creates even more liquidity.

At the simplest level, central banks, by holding and recycling dollars (and to a lesser degree, euros and yen), are a significant part of the pyramid's stability as well as being a source of funds (Figure 37).

The perception of the dollar as a stable store of wealth is the *sine qua non* of being acceptable asset money. The liquidity pyramid would destruct overnight were central bankers to dump the dollar. This would happen despite the fact that central banks' international reserves are only a modest part of the total available liquidity in the pyramid.

As international trade expands, transaction demand grows for the currencies of the liquidity pyramid, for some more than for others. This adds to the stability of those currencies and thus increases their usability in the liquidity pyramid as asset money. This does not prevent one currency in the liquidity pyramid devaluing against another. The yen did so for a long

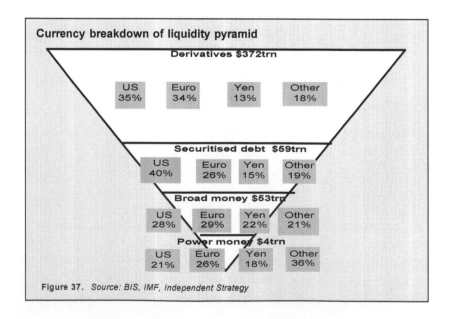

Figure 37. *Source: BIS, IMF, Independent Strategy*

time. But currencies moved along a trend (weaker or stronger) with very low volatility. This means the pyramid is stable.

In another way too the liquidity function can defuse volatility from imbalances in the real economy. The over-supply of the dollar, a function of US economic imbalances, is absorbed by two demand factors: investment demand in the liquidity pyramid; and transaction demand from the real economy.

At the very least, this points to two conclusions. One is that the New Monetarism party can go on longer because 'real' economic demand for the currencies that form the liquidity pyramid lends stability to the whole structure. The other is that when the party ends, currency turmoil could either be a cause or an effect of the ensuing liquidity contraction, but it will for sure be a part of it, as the twin systems of trade and asset markets start to reject the weakest dominant currency — the dollar.

CHAPTER FIVE

Bubbles and the global savings glut

One of the mysteries of New Monetarism is that rising policy interest rates had no effect on controlling the expansion of liquidity for a very long time. This was because increases in short-term rates did not cascade into the pricing of the bigger longer-term tranches in the liquidity pyramid.

In the US economy, derivatives have been used to 'freeze', at historically low interest rates, $50trn of capital or five years of GDP, as measured by the notional value of the credits represented by the interest-rate swaps. This delays the impact of Fed rate hikes. Increases in central bank interest rates remained stuck in the small, narrow apex of the pyramid occupied by central bank and short-term money. That is why liquidity continued to expand even when the Fed was hiking interest rates.

By August 2007, according to the Fed, it had removed the exceptional easing of monetary conditions that followed 9/11. Real Fed interest rates, by most measures, returned to their long-term mean (Figure 38). But if one computes the cost of money

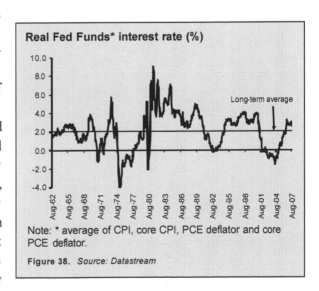

Real Fed Funds* interest rate (%)

Long-term average

Note: * average of CPI, core CPI, PCE deflator and core PCE deflator.

Figure 38. *Source: Datastream*

using the interest rates that are used to price credit throughout the liquidity pyramid, particularly in its upper reaches, Fed tightening has had less of an effect.

This is hardly surprising, as the wider tranches of the pyramid do not use central bank money. Furthermore, the growth in derivatives is overridingly in maturities beyond one year and are thus they are relatively unaffected by changes in Fed Fund rates that leave longer term rates at lower or little changed levels.

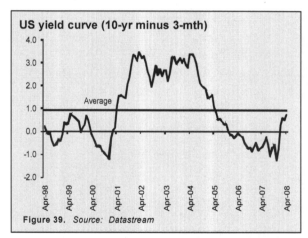

Figure 39. *Source: Datastream*

Another way of analysing the cost of money throughout the pyramid is through the yield curve. As central banks raised policy interest rates, or threatened to do so, long-term bond yields did not follow or even fell. So yield curves flattened or inverted, meaning that, as short-term money cost more, longer-term money cost the same or less (Figure 39)!

A lot of theories have been proffered on why this happened and what it means. An inverted yield curve can presage a recession. But, as the economies of US, Japan and Europe were all motoring, this seemed unlikely at the time.

Another explanation is that the shrinking supply of long-term bonds issued by governments, together with the need for pension funds to match the maturity of assets and liabilities, increased demand for long-term securitised paper and lowered long-term bond yields.

That may be at least part of the explanation why bond yields were so low. It explains some flatness in the yield curve, particularly in the UK. But it is too small a factor to justify it globally or even in the US. Moreover, pension funds have to match the return on assets and liabilities as much as their maturities. Today's low real rates raise doubts about pension funds' ability to achieve this when investments in long-term debt yield so little.

The global savings glut

Then some high-placed US officials argued that it was a global savings glut that kept long-term money cheap in the US, hinting that it could do so forever.

Fed Chair Ben Bernanke presented this theory of a global savings glut. It runs like this. The world is awash with surplus savings, principally in Asian emerging markets. These surplus savings flow into the US. This produces an equilibrium whereby the US has to save less and spend more to offset Asia's excessive thrift. The US was performing a great service to the world by consuming the excess thrift of Asia which otherwise would have become a global deflationary gap *a la* Keynes. The theory posits that the existence of this Asian savings surplus kept down US real long-term interest rates and would do so for a very long time.

The sub-optimal bit of this equilibrium, according to Bernanke is that the US and other ageing societies should really be saving more and so run current account surpluses and capital account deficits, as they invest in emerging markets, in order to finance their dotage. But, according to Bernanke, there is a very low risk of disruptive adjustment from this deficiency.

On the face of it, Bernanke's argument is just another version of the old shibboleth that it is the capital account surplus of the US that creates the current account deficit. It is capital flowing into the US, as the most attractive global investment destination, that obliges the US to consume so much and save so little.

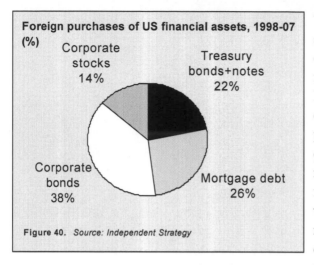

Foreign purchases of US financial assets, 1998-07 (%)

Corporate stocks 14%

Treasury bonds+notes 22%

Corporate bonds 38%

Mortgage debt 26%

Figure 40. *Source: Independent Strategy*

That thesis can be skittled, when you consider that US financial assets no longer offer foreign investors superior returns. Indeed, foreign money mostly flows into relatively lower-return, relatively unproductive US treasuries and mortgage instruments (Figure 40).

Anyway, surely the fall in the dollar's trade-weighted index over the last three years is proof enough that the *ex post* widening of the US current account deficit is not created by an *ex ante* inflow of foreign capital? If it had, the dollar would be appreciating, not declining.

The very idea of a global savings glut has to be based on speculation (not evidence) about the *ex ante* intentions of savers and investors. *Ex post*, the world's savings and investments always balance, as witnessed by the fact that the world's current and capital account balances net out to zero (bar some significant statistical discrepancies).

Also Bernanke argues that it is the Asian central banks/authorities that have forced people to save more than local investment needs in the last six years. Apparently, the central banks act as intermediaries between Asian savers and the US in order to accumulate more dollar reserves as a war chest against any future crisis like they experienced in 1997.

In reality, the causal chain runs the other way: with excess US consumption creating current account surpluses in Asian economies. Then these excess dollars have to be reinvested through the hands of passive Asian central bank players (Figure 41).

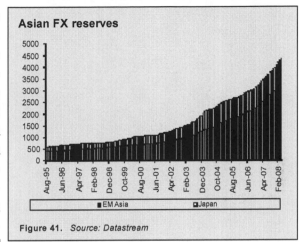

Asian FX reserves

■ EM Asia   □ Japan

Figure 41. *Source: Datastream*

Let's focus upon the argument that is used to support Bernanke's key conclusion. In a nutshell, Bernanke wants to show that it is Asian surplus savings that have held down US long bond rates. Therefore the Fed is not to blame for abnormally-low interest rates. Moreover, long-term interest rates will stay low for as long as Asia's savings remain excessive, i.e. a very long time, in Bernanke's view. So there is no systemic risk from a credit bubble collapse.

Bernanke does not justify his conclusion by any statistical analysis. Moreover, he demotes any other possible factor that could have kept real interest rates low (like lower risk premiums as inflation falls) to a footnote.

When you drop some analytical acid on the evidence, you find that the current account surpluses of Asia and OPEC (equivalent to their surplus of savings over investment) explain just 15% of the decline in US long-term real interest rates in the last 20 years. It was disinflation that did the

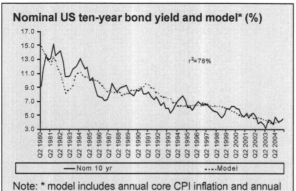

Note: * model includes annual core CPI inflation and annual supply growth in 10-year plus bonds

Figure 42. *Source: Datastream*

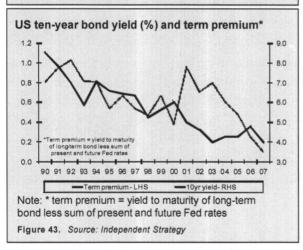

Note: * term premium = yield to maturity of long-term bond less sum of present and future Fed rates

Figure 43. *Source: Independent Strategy*

job — disinflation and the shrinking supply of longer-dated US treasuries explained 78% of the decline in US long-term interest rates (Figure 42).

The main cause of low long-term interest rates was that investors were simply extraordinarily optimistic about long-term inflation (Figure 43).

Think of a ten-year US treasury bond: what is the risk of investing in it? There is no material risk of default. The US government can always print money to pay its debts. The risk is that inflation will erode the value of your investment.

To compensate for this risk, long-term bond markets pay you a 'risk premium' for inflation called a 'term premium'. This is the additional yield on a long-term US treasury bond over the sum of current and future short-term (Fed) interest rates during the life of the bond.

Imagine that you thought that the Fed would always be behind the curve and would keep its interest rates below inflation. You would want long-term bond rates to be higher than present and future Fed rates to make up for this. So the bond's term premium would rise. The same would be true if you thought that inflation would be more volatile during the life of the bond. That would raise the risk that your income over the period you held the bond would be worth less in real terms or that if you were to sell at a bad time, you would get less than the par value that the US government must pay you on maturity.

Over the last decade, bond markets became increasingly optimistic that inflation would stay low and stable. Investors reduced the inflation risk premium on US treasuries accordingly. This was the major reason why the weighted cost of capital in the liquidity pyramid went so low. Excess corporate savings that flow into financial markets and reduced offerings of long-term US treasuries were the others.

The combination of the end of disinflation and shrinking corporate net savings will be a double blow to financial assets. The combination will lower returns and increase volatility.

Bernanke and others attribute the emergence of the global savings glut to a rise in emerging Asian economies' savings rates. Yet, in aggregate, savings rates in emerging Asia fell after 1997, despite a rise in China's and have risen only slightly since 2003 (again mainly almost completely due to China). All in all, over the whole period, they were flat. In reality, like the

BUBBLES AND THE GLOBAL SAVINGS GLUT

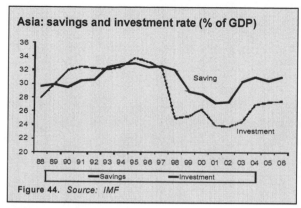

Figure 44. *Source: IMF*

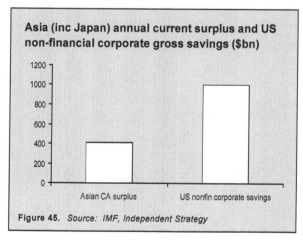

Figure 45. *Source: IMF, Independent Strategy*

OECD, emerging Asia had a corporate savings glut caused by falling investment, not by rising savings rates (Figure 44).

Moreover, Asia's excess corporate savings amounts to only 40% of the excess savings of the US corporate sector (Figure 45).

As emerging Asia's excess savings rates got voluntarily invested in US assets (as the liquidity pyramid says they should), they were material in keeping the dollar stable, but less important in setting US long-term interest rates. Rather than a global savings glut we should talk about a corporate dearth of investment that may be a hangover from the excess investment of the dot.com bubble and so a lot less durable than is widely appreciated.

We find that the global savings glut is a product of a cyclical rise in corporate surplus savings (defined as net cash flow less investment), which will diminish when the economic cycle turns or cost inflation starts to eat into today's astronomical margins, causing profits to revert to the mean as percentage of national income.

BUBBLES AND THE GLOBAL SAVINGS GLUT

In sum, the 'autistic' recycling of dollars from Asia was vital to the stability of the dollar and thus to its dominant role in the liquidity pyramid. Just imagine what would happen if all the Asian countries dumped their dollars. But Asia's surplus savings play a lesser role in keeping US long-term interest rates low.

New paradigms

It is tempting to view the world's imbalances (Asia's surplus and America's dearth of savings) as the result of a new economic order whereby the rich economies become shopping malls filled with rich countries' old age pensioners and the emerging economies produce everything for the malls to merchandise and invest their economic gains (current account surplus) to build more shopping malls in rich countries.

But there is a much simpler monetary explanation that can explain all of this in terms of cash flows rather than new economic architecture. New Monetarism, by creating massive global liquidity, acted like oil in an old jalopy: it keeps it running for a while even though it's half bust.

As Japan exported cheap capital in search of higher yield, the US offered the world higher-yielding bonds than most, even if those yields were low by historical standards. Money flowed to the US, which kept the dollar up and US liquidity booming.

This is not a story about the economic surplus of emerging markets opting for investment in the superior productivity and returns of corporate America. It is a simple story of cash surpluses chasing higher yields (often of securities with very low capital productivity, such as a mortgage-backed securities and CDOs)!

In 2005 and 2006, the highest yields in town were in the US. Money flowed there, keeping the dollar relatively stable by covering the US current account deficit. But this bloated the US financial system with liquidity that drove up asset prices, so keeping the US consumer borrowing and shopping and buying from Asia.

BUBBLES AND THE GLOBAL SAVINGS GLUT

In contrast, dollars were flowing in so fast into China (from export earnings and capital flows) that the country, with an economy half the size of Japan's, now has more international reserves than any other in the world.

Normally, such dollar inflows would cause the recipient's currency to rocket. But the Chinese don't want that. So the dollars were exchanged for renminbi by the central bank and then flood into domestic liquidity, while the dollars were reinvested by the monetary authorities back into the US. To do anything else, such as the central bank selling dollars into other currencies, would upset the mercantile Chinese apple cart by making its currency and exports to all dollar trade areas more expensive.

So the world economy appeared to move forward seamlessly. But this was not because there was some new economic paradigm out there — it was just rather a lot of excess liquidity.

CHAPTER SIX

The magic of capitalism

Hernando de Soto in his book, *The mystery of capital,* had one simple idea. He believed that the 'magic of capitalism' can only be unleashed by the establishment of a legal society that creates title to property. When property can be protected, it can be exchanged and used to raise capital efficiently.

The magic of capitalism occurs when a physical asset can at the same time become a financial asset and be turned into money (Figure 46). Thus, in De Soto's view, economic underdevelopment is closely correlated with how long it takes to transact property.

Put it this way. A Thai massage shack on a beach may be a productive asset for a family. But as long as the family can't own title to it, sell all or part of that title or borrow against it, it just remains a productive asset and not a financial one. When the Xmas 2005 *tsunami* wiped out hundreds of thousands of these poor people and their businesses, GDP in the affected countries was practically unchanged. Why? Because these 'small' peo-

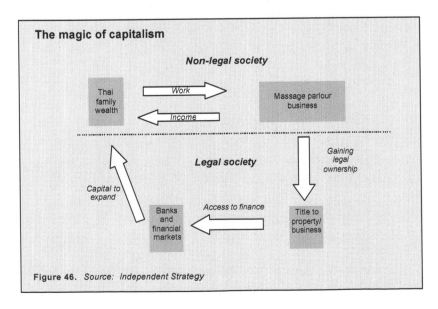

Figure 46. *Source: Independent Strategy*

ple and their businesses had never existed within the official economy, even though they probably constitute its backbone.

Emerging and submerging markets (and what makes them so) may provide the best proof of De Soto's law today. But a glance back through history teaches us that the US economy only took off with the codification of land ownership and the UK's with the establishment of limited partnerships. Good property law is the quintessential ingredient of good economies.

One reason communism failed (and why capitalism fails today just as abysmally) in many poor countries is that people are deprived of property rights, either by ideology or corruption. They are locked into their businesses but their ability to grow them, diversify their assets, sell their business and advance their own well-being is curtailed. That is why micro-finance is such a brilliant concept, as it empowers the tiny asset values of small businesses.

If we may make an extension to De Soto's thinking, it is to add the concept of liquidity and particularly that of asset money. The minute that a productive asset becomes a financial asset, the concept of asset money has entered the economy: financial market liquidity has been created.

This liquidity, in turn, creates the second chapter of the value of the asset: wealth. It is only at that point that the value of the asset becomes more than a stream of income, more than just a business to earn the family's daily bread. Instead, the asset begets a second value, a capital value based on its discounted future income, which can be sold in whole or in part or borrowed against. Only then does the asset become wealth.

Defining and measuring bubbles

The 'liquidity pyramid' merely symbolises a mechanical arrangement, albeit complex, of financial intermediaries and markets — exactly those that add the ingredient of magic to de Soto's capitalism.

How do we judge if the cornucopia of asset money we describe is an inherent source of future financial instability of a magnitude that would seriously hurt the global economy? In other words, at what point does the white magic of de Soto's mystery of capital become the black magic of credit excess and asset bubbles?

According to seminal research at the Bank of International Settlements, when credit growth is significantly above trend, it is a very good indicator of financial or economic crises to come (Figures 47 & 48). BIS researchers found that when credit growth is 4-5 percentage points above trend or asset prices are 40-50% above trend, this predicted nearly 80% of financial crises within a time horizon of one to three years (Figure 47).

Although BIS researchers used a more traditional definition of liquidity than we do (basing their study on money aggregates), it still makes sense that too much money chasing too few assets is the *Ursprung* of all financial crises.

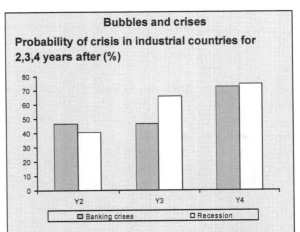

Bubbles and crises

Probability of crisis in industrial countries for 2,3,4 years after (%)

□ Banking crises   □ Recession

BIS researchers, Borio and Lowe, looked at the long-term relationship between credit growth in the G10 economies and the movement of asset prices. They found that there were 38 crisis episodes between 1970 and 1999 spread over 27 countries. They found that when credit as a % of GDP grew to 4-5% points above trend, it was followed by some form of financial crisis on nearly 80% of occasions within one year. When several factors are combined (credit, asset prices and the exchange-rate), the probability of a crisis (either banking or economic) was still around 40% two years out and around 70% four years out.

Figure 47. *Source: BIS*

THE MAGIC OF CAPITALISM

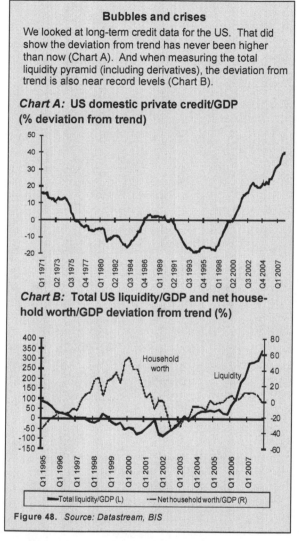

Bubbles and crises

We looked at long-term credit data for the US. That did show the deviation from trend has never been higher than now (Chart A). And when measuring the total liquidity pyramid (including derivatives), the deviation from trend is also near record levels (Chart B).

Chart A: US domestic private credit/GDP (% deviation from trend)

Chart B: Total US liquidity/GDP and net household worth/GDP deviation from trend (%)

Household worth

Liquidity

—— Total liquidity/GDP (L) ·—— Net household worth/GDP (R)

Figure 48. *Source: Datastream, BIS*

Applying this model in 2007 indicated that we were into dangerous waters in the US (Figure 48A). Modifying the definition of credit to include securitised debt and derivatives reinforced that message (Figure 48B).

But if excess credit is the cause of financial crisis, then it must first manifest itself in asset bubbles — right? Defining a bubble is a good place to answer that.

Charles Kindleberger is recognised as 'Mr Bubble' among economists. The Kindleberger definition of a bubble is "a sharp rise in price of an asset or a range of assets in a continuous process, with the initial rise generating expectations of further rises and attracting new buyers — generally speculators interested in profits from trading in the asset rather than its use or earning capacity".

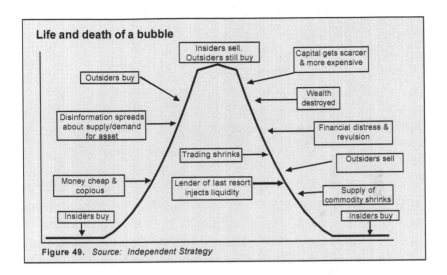

Figure 49. *Source: Independent Strategy*

The life of a bubble can can also be charted (Figure 49). If the BIS model is right, we should have been somewhere near the peak in 2007 with abnormal high returns on a variety of assets and high turnover based on increasingly flimsy stories.

Double bubbles and reefs

Back in early 2007, we trawled the great financial seas for asset bubbles. We looked for assets where 1) valuations are much higher than fundamentals warranted; 2) trading volumes were abnormally high; 3) returns were off the map. We did this and came up with no significant bubbles in equities or bonds and only a few in housing, commodity or energy markets!

How come there were so few bubbles if both traditionally-defined credit in the US and the liquidity pyramid globally were expanding at double-digit rates (well above trend) and the cost of capital was still well below the natural rate?

The answer lies in the existence of 'reefs' as opposed to 'bubbles'. Reefs are financial disequilibria that are hidden from view due to the high level of liquidity, but have serious consequences for the real economy when liquidity ebbs (Figure 50). The characteristic of a reef is that, to the extent that excess liquidity permeates all the drivers of the economy, the less bubbles will appear and the greater will be the economic damage that will be inflicted by a reversal of the 'credit' cycle.

Its lesson is clear: if the tide of liquidity lifts all economic boats proportionately, then their individual relative valuations to each other will not appear unreasonable (Figure 51). All that is needed to maintain an aura of reason is for the 'credit cycle' to boost asset prices, wealth, economic activity, income and profit at the same time and proportionately (i.e. preserving traditional valuation cross-relationships).

If this happens, valuations will not signal the existence of bubbles. Instead of being reassuring, this indicates that the dangers are more widespread, affecting a greater number of economic variables. If the increase in asset values were the result of factor productivity gains rather than liquidity, the

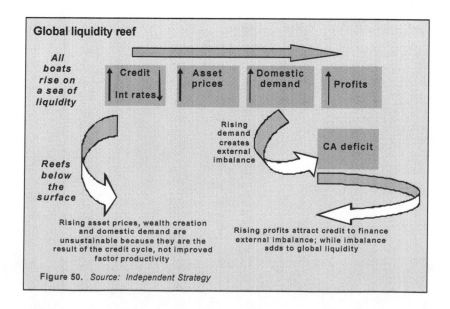

Figure 50. *Source: Independent Strategy*

boost to the economy would be rock solid. But if it were down to leverage and liquidity, then, although relative valuations may not signal bubbles, it is likely that economic imbalances like a current account deficit will.

History offers some evidence that this theory of reefs works in reality. IMF research indicates that only one-third of a wide range of stock market crashes since 1800 were associated with a previous bubble. Yet 50% of equity crashes were associated with recessions.

All bubbles (and reefs) are financed by copious credit. In Kindleberger's words, the process (of creating new forms of money and credit) is end-less: "fix any 'M' and the market will create new forms of money in periods of boom to get around the limit and create the necessity to fix a new variable M1". In the words of the 19th century commentator, Walter Bagehot, "men of business in England do not like the currency question. They are perplexed to define accurately what money is: how to count they know, but what to count they do not know".

In order for bubbles and reefs to develop, credit must be plentiful. But it need not be cheap (in either real or nominal terms) judged by historical

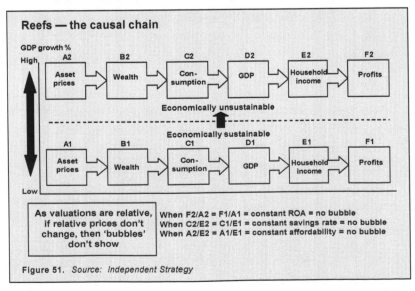

Figure 51. *Source: Independent Strategy*

standards. Investors need only be convinced that credit is cheap relative to forecast gains on the assets they invest in.

In other words, credit need only be cheap when deflated by anticipated asset price inflation. Asset price inflation may be totally divorced from consumer prices throughout the bubble period, the former being high and the latter often being low. A case in point was the Japanese bubble economy of the 1980s.

Today, most long-term bond yields are low by historical standards. Yet bond market returns to investors are way below levels that normally characterise a bubble. This is typical of a reef valuation — excessively priced historically, but stable and with little evidence of 'mania'.

Consequently, successful pursuit of stable and low consumer price inflation by central banks is not synonymous with eschewing asset price bubbles or achieving financial stability. Bubbles and reefs thrive in the calm waters of low or falling inflation.

Low and stable inflation can engender excessive liquidity because it boosts the confidence of individuals and corporations to take on more leverage. And leverage is liquidity. In so far as the leverage is used to target asset prices, asset prices will rise as a consequence without any improvement in fundamentals such as productivity.

If asset markets rise because people have confidence in 'fundamentals', the result will be the creation of wealth and more confidence. This will be borrowed against (or assets will be liquidated or equity withdrawn) and spent, thus boosting economic activity and profits. Thus rising asset prices lift all relative prices, profits and activity proportionately, hiding the reef underneath.

Low inflation can also create overconfidence in the conduct of monetary policy — that interest rates will remain low forever — or that central bankers have permanently modified human behaviour.

The Japanese bubble economy grew like Topsy, while CPI inflation fell or stayed low (interest rates were relatively high, but falling). The Nikkei took off in early 1986 as the CPI index moved into negative territory. The Nikkei only cracked when inflation moved up towards 4% in 1989. Nominal bond yields were still near decade lows when the Nikkei burst.

Liquidity and valuations

What does the cheapness of credit do to asset valuations? Take two US examples: equities and housing. If equities are valued using current long-term interest rates to discount profits, they appear undervalued. However, if the exercise is redone using a 'normalised' (20-year long-term average) bond yield, equities appear overvalued.

The same goes for housing at the peak of the US housing bubble. If affordability was calculated using mortgage rates, a house could look cheap. But if the price of the same house were compared to buyers' income or the rent it could command, it looked expensive.

That is why the bulls were declaring US housing not to be a bubble (finding the usual 'fundamentals' to justify their views — like Latino immigration). The bears, on the other hand, comparing house prices to income, claimed housing was overpriced for equally fundamental reasons.

In reality, the bulls were seeking to justify overpriced housing by reference to underpriced capital. Thus one bubble made another's valuation look reasonable. This is the 'double-bubble valuation jeopardy', which is a kernel fallacy in the absence of 'bubbles' in financial reef conditions.

CHAPTER SEVEN

Liquidity and financial asset volatility

It is time to bring volatility into the equation. Between 2000 and 2007 the volatility of financial markets fell dramatically and to levels not seen since the mid-1990s (Figure 52). Derivative spreads, particularly for those that offer insurance against changes in interest rates (e.g. swaps) and against default (CDSs), collapsed. Currency volatility for developed and undeveloped economies dropped too.

Low volatility increases the self-generating capacity of the liquidity pyramid. Take just three examples. Low volatility may decrease the cost of buying insurance in derivative markets. If it costs

Volatility			
Equity markets since 1959	**US**	**Jap**	**Ger**
Mean volatility (% pts)	13.19	14.13	16.78
Volatility in H1'07	10.07	13.66	12.77
Bond markets since 1986	**US**	**Jap**	**Ger**
Mean volatility (% pts)	4.48	3.14	3.26
Volatility in H1'07	3.88	1.94	2.94
Currency markets since 1971	**Jap**	**Ger**	**UK**
(% vs dollar)			
Mean volatility	9.39	9.70	8.61
Volatility in H1'07	9.20	8.81	8.27

Figure 52. *Source: IMF*

less to do so, the financial sector will buy more insurance (against default and rising rates). By removing most of these risks (collateral risk remains) from the balance sheet, financial intermediaries can create new credit because their stock of risk assets to their equity and reserves is held down relative to their rising loan book. Much of which may also be securitised and 'sold' off banks' balance sheets.

On a wider scale, the low cost of locking in a stable cost of financing, using instruments such as interest-rate swaps, will encourage more players to inoculate their business against a future rise in rates. Again, this facilitates higher levels of leverage, not only in non-financial corporations, but also in the leveraged buyout and private equity sectors.

LIQUIDITY AND FINANCIAL ASSET VOLATILITY

Finally, a significant part of the creation of liquidity in the pyramid relies upon borrowing in one asset — normally a low-yielding one — and investing in another higher-yielding one. A Japanese bank investing yen deposits in US treasuries is doing just that. Doing so adds to US liquidity without currently diminishing Japan's because bank deposits in Japan were fallow money that no one wanted to borrow. So lending it to Uncle Sam did not change Japan's liquidity.

But if anything raises volatility durably, the impact on liquidity would be severe because of the engineering of the liquidity pyramid, which depends for its stability, expansion and returns upon low volatility, low inflation and cost of capital. This impact would be quite independent of the cause of increased volatility.

To assess the risk of higher volatility we should first look at why it has fallen in recent years. First, greater macro economic stability (often referred to as the Great Moderation) — the volatility of economies (growth, inflation, interest rates etc) fell by as much as financial market volatility (but earlier).

Second, more targeted and more transparent monetary policy management also made for less financial market shocks. Third, there was more stable corporate performance and improved profitability, due to productivity gains from better resource utilisation, lower leverage and better inventory management etc.

And finally, there were financial factors. Improved liquidity and risk dispersion due to new market participants (e.g. hedge funds specialising in insurance products) and new products (e.g. derivatives such as CDOs, CDSs etc) allowed market participants to be seen to unbundle, hedge and disperse risk throughout the financial system (the US mortgage backed security (MBS) and derivatives based on them being the single largest example). Of course, much of this was perception rather than reality, but that perception is what mattered at the time.

LIQUIDITY AND FINANCIAL ASSET VOLATILITY

Recent research downplays the impact of the macroeconomic Great Moderation because it happened much earlier than the corresponding fall in volatility in financial markets. On the other hand, the idea that financial factors are at least partially responsible for low financial market volatility means that it is the architecture of the liquidity pyramid itself that creates the low volatility, upon which it depends for much of its ability to generate liquidity!

To explain this process further, follow the wheels of fortune from left to right (Figure 53). In the first wheel, we see the three drivers of lower volatility: the great moderation (macroeconomic); new derivative insurance products; and improved central bank policy. This drives the second wheel of better risk distribution, lower financial market volatility and, consequently, higher risk appetite. This moves the third wheel to higher leverage and more liquidity. In the fourth wheel, asset prices rise due to more liquidity chasing them and returns per unit of risk improve. This feeds back into higher risk appetite and the process starts again.

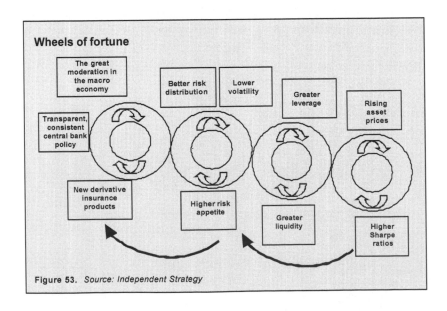

Figure 53. *Source: Independent Strategy*

LIQUIDITY AND FINANCIAL ASSET VOLATILITY

Before pooh poohing the idea, it is as well to remember that in the course of the last five years the financial system has weathered umpteen macro and micro shocks with hardly a tremor. Until the credit crisis broke, the regulators' contention has proven correct that derivatives diminish systemic risk in the financial system by removing concentrated risk from banks and spreading it among multiple players more willing, if not always better equipped, to handle it.

Our own view, to echo Hyman Minsky, is that there is nothing more likely to produce instability than a lengthy period of stability. At the peak of the bull market, much of the pricing of credit and other capital was grossly out of kilter with risk, including that for credit derivatives and much of the financing of leverage buyouts, private equity deals, commodities and emerging market bonds.

Up to mid-2007, risk, the main determinant of the liquidity multiplier, was still being grossly underpriced. Volatility measures for financial asset prices were close to their lows and Japanese banks and currency derivative markets continue to fund the yen carry trade (Figure 54). The pricing of 'tail risk' (the risk of a multi-standard deviation from the average pricing of a financial market or asset) remained supremely optimistic.

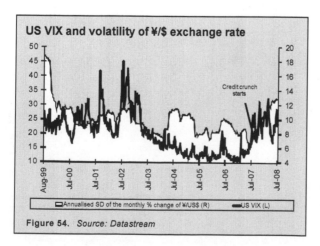

Figure 54. *Source: Datastream*

Markets were commensurately confident that the economic and credit cycle pose no threats. CDS rates, for example, were only a little higher than their cyclical lows. US and

LIQUIDITY AND FINANCIAL ASSET VOLATILITY

Euro banking sector willingness to lend was still at or close to boom readings.

Two things can be said about this. Random walk was back; markets believed the best forecast for tomorrow is yesterday (and all our yesterdays were of low volatility and disinflation). But, as Macbeth put it, "all our yesterdays have lighted fools the way to dusty death".

Second, there was a high degree of market confidence that extreme outcomes of any sort are highly improbable. All of this created a circular logic: risk appetite contributed to financial market stability, which, in turn, boosted risk appetite that created financial market stability.

But there is one really interesting thing about the lack of volatility that so many financial assets shared: their price movements were becoming much more highly correlated as they became less volatile. This is like the uniform view of the aged arrayed upon serried ranks of deck chairs on a beach. When it comes to the time of dying they will all die at more or less the same time.

The lack of volatility was just the quiet before the storm. And because diverse financial assets had seen their price movements become more closely correlated, there were few benefits of risk diversification when markets turn sour. They all fell together.

Nature (or human behaviour) does not follow Art (or the tranquility produced by financial engineering) so faithfully forever. In the end, humans are volatile and so is nature; every seventh wave is a big one and when it breaks, central bankers become as King Canute, awash in a disobedient sea of their own undoing. And so it was from August 2007.

CHAPTER EIGHT

Reversing the liquidity cycle

To recap our story so far: New Monetarism claims that the global liquidity pyramid was shaped and sized by forces that were limited or non-existent in previous cycles. The quantity and price of money were no longer controlled by central banks. Central bank-dictated reserve ratios no longer set the credit multiplier. And hefting policy rates did not affect the cost of capital throughout the pyramid.

In the old days, liquidity was set by the reserve ratios of the central banks and the size of their power money. So total liquidity equalled power money multiplied the inverse of the reserve ratio. But now no longer!

Liquidity has no reference in the majority of its components to central bank power money. It was now a function of more abstract entities like: risk appetite (which sets leverage); currency carry trades (which help set quantity); derivatives (which set risk); and market — rather than policy — interest rates (which set demand).

As long as the cost of capital remained below the natural rate of interest (which is the rate of interest at which savings equals productive rather than speculative investment), the liquidity pyramid expanded more or less at the rate of demand for asset money (which can indifferently be a function of real investment demand or speculation) — Figure 55.

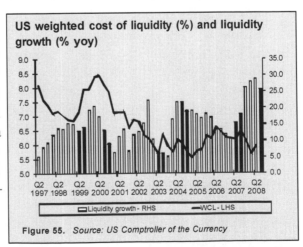

US weighted cost of liquidity (%) and liquidity growth (% yoy)

Liquidity growth - RHS   WCL - LHS

Figure 55. *Source: US Comptroller of the Currency*

REVERSING THE LIQUIDITY CYCLE

But once the cost of long-term capital rises above the natural interest rate, the liquidity pyramid to contract sharply if the expansion and contraction phrases were to be symmetrical. If asset bubbles start to collapse, central banks, being unable to bear the economic cost (i.e. guilt), would act asymmetrically.

Between 2002 and 2007, central banks raised interest rates either to 'normalise' them from post 9/11 easy monetary policy, or to combat inflation. But at the first sign of asset price deflation, they eased precipitously. Thus any pain of being invested in an asset bubble would be of short duration. This reinforced the markets' conviction that global monetary policy was asymmetric and biased in favour of investors and speculators.

There is also another assymetric correction. The market believed that even if central bankers over-tightened monetary policy, killed the economy and created deflation, making real yields rise, it would not harm the asset (bond) price permanently (e.g. the bond holder would get his money back).

This is logical, but wrong. It's true that today corporations have little excess debt and governments will always pay up. But this ignores the impact of falling profit margins and the rising cost of capital when the liquidity cycle contracts. Indeed, yields on bonds and many other assets were so low that the only reason to invest (and forego current consumption to do so) was if asset prices inflated further. That needed more and more liquidity to buy the existing stock of assets at ever higher prices.

This was the logic of the US treasury market. As the bond market set the pricing of much of long-term capital and was thus the fount at which all other asset bubbles drink, this logic was self-fulfilling: it was true for as long as it was true.

Of course, truth is not forever — as most divorcees who once said "I love you forever" know. The liquidity cycle, as defined by New Monetarism, was bound to reverse too. That reversal could be due to a sharp rise in the cost of capital; the demise of the yen carry trade or through some

Asset prices and the cost of capital

Do asset price bubbles need the catalyst of a rising cost of capital before they burst? History shows that sometimes they do and sometimes they don't. Or more precisely, sometimes falling asset prices *coincide* with a rising cost of capital and some times they don't. So asset price bubbles can be pricked by the pin (or knife) of rising interest rates or they can be stretched so far that they burst of their own accord. Chart A shows that the Great Crash of 1929 took place in an environment of low and falling interest rates. Similarly, the Hong Kong property bust of 1993 coincided with falling interest rates (Chart B). In contrast, interest rates were on the rise when the great Nikkei bubble burst at the end of 1989 (Chart C) and when the Nasdaq burst in 2000 (Chart D).

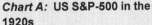

Chart A: **US S&P-500 in the 1920s**

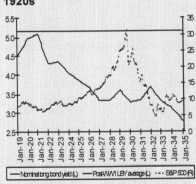

Chart B: **Hong Kong nominal 3-mth interest rate and property prices (% yoy)**

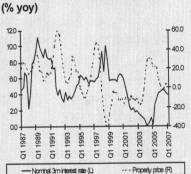

Chart C: **Japan Nikkei-225 in the 1990s**

Chart D: **US Nasdaq in the 1990s**

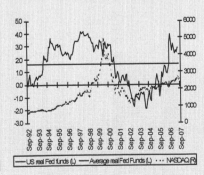

Figure 56. *Source: Robert J Shiller, Datastream, Independent Strategy*

major geopolitical accident. The events that would cause liquidity to contract were close encounters of a daily kind.

But it could just happen like spontaneous combustion. Most financial crises that result in recession or depression are not preceded by easily identifiable bubbles or bursts, just an excessive credit cycle (see Figure 56 on page 77). The collapse happens simply: one day people come to market and the pigs are too dear. So they stop buying pigs. And so it was. One day, Americans just stopped buying houses at ever rising prices.

The reversal of New Monetarism's first liquidity cycle began with some small seismic shocks before the credit crunch erupted in August 2007. There were market shakes in May 2006 and in February 2007. They were dismissed as one-off events and rapidly disposed of by markets. But both periods were rehearsals of what would happen to the global credit cycle as the collateral damage from the collapse of the US housing market began to materialise.

Conclusion

What all this tells us is that the new forms of money or liquidity that came to dominate the macroeconomic and financial world were not here to stay. They were a product of serendipity or a fortuous combination of events — namely, the twin decades of disinflation, US political and economic dominance; the economic rise of China; and the dissaving of America's households.

None of these phenomena would be here for eternity or even for more than a few decades. In the case of disinflation, US dominance and American household spending, their days were already over. That's why we were not in any 'new paradigm'. The bubbles of New Monetarism would eventually burst (starting with US housing). And the flows of liquidity would eventually break the banks of the weirs they are held in and then dry up.

CHAPTER NINE

Parched world

One year later, the global credit crunch is still not over. But when it is, it won't spell the end of capitalism. So what will happen over the next decade or so?

Credit crunch and imbalances

Credit, as measured by our liquidity pyramid, will continue to contract and economic activity with it, for at least another year (Figure 57). The reasons are

Figure 57. *Source: Independent Strategy*

that the sub-prime crisis is a small part of the total problem of excess debt, but sufficiently important to induce recession in the OECD economies.

The recession will bring out the other credit problems. The result will be to damage severely the capital base of financial intermediaries and so curtail their ability to create credit for a considerable period (Figure 58).

Global bank losses and credit growth

We forecast losses from the crunch in credit markets to reach $607bn for the banks and $724bn for the non-deposit financial institutions. After taking into account new equity capital raised so far by financial institutions, we reckon that the banks will suffer a shortfall of another $281bn and the NDFIs another $264bn.

Even if global financial institutions use likely future earnings over the next 12 months to cover these further losses, they will still suffer net capital destruction of $191bn.

At current levels of leverage (9-10 times), that would be equivalent to a contraction of credit of $1.7trn, or 5-7% of total credit expected by mid-2009. It would mean global credit (loans and debt) would be flat or fall from here over the next 12 months. Global liquidity, which includes derivatives, would fall by 10-20%.

Figure 58. *Source: Independent Strategy*

When the crunch is over, credit growth and leverage will still play a much smaller role in driving GDP growth in the next decade than they have done in the last.

Regulatory change and risk appetite will dictate that financial intermediaries will have to grow more of their loans 'on balance sheet'. And they will have to make more provisions for 'off balance sheet' credit. All this will use up lending capacity and require increased reserves.

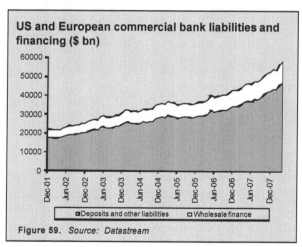

US and European commercial bank liabilities and financing ($ bn)

□ Deposits and other liabilities   □ Wholesale finance

Figure 59. *Source: Datastream*

Dollar increase in debt required to make a $1 increase in US real GDP (5-yr rolling average)

Figure 60. *Source: Datastream*

It's curtains for the business model (borrowing short and lending long) that relied on wholesale financing — Figure 59. The shift in risk appetite and regulatory changes will make it impossible for banks to finance growth in this way.

As the OECD economies have become habituated to using more and more debt per unit of extra GDP (Figure 60), shrinking credit will set up a reinforcing loop of poor growth and ongoing financial sector impairment that will take several years to resolve. No action by central banks can reverse this process.

There have been long periods when the US debt to GDP ratios was fairly constant and the economy did well. But that was when the US national savings rate was relatively high and capital from households was channelled into productive investment in a balanced way through the banks and equity markets without creating multiple layers of gearing.

But in the last two decades, the US national savings rate collapsed and the funding it traditonally supplied for investment became replaced by gearing (Figure 61). Increased leverage was facilitated by securitisation and the increasing importance of new financial business models and entities, such as transaction-oriented financial intermediation and non-deposit-taking financial intermediaries (NDFIs).

There is a well-argued view that the explosion of leverage per unit of GDP indicates that increased debt had little impact on GDP (which is why it rocketed as a proportion of it) and thus neither will credit contraction. What most of the increase in debt did was to finance the shuffling of non-productive assets and the title to them, not additional output in the 'real' economy. So this view is the reverse of our thinking that each marginal unit of GDP needs more and more units of credit.

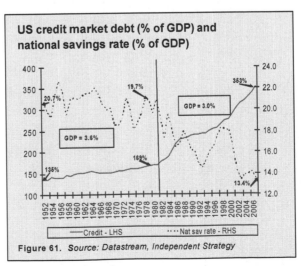

Figure 61. *Source: Datastream, Independent Strategy*

81

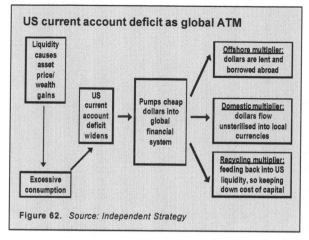

Figure 62. *Source: Independent Strategy*

Our view is that, as leverage is reduced, capital will get scarcer and more costly. This will damage investment. There will also be less liquidity to drive up asset prices. That will reduce consumption by depressing confidence and reducing the means of financing spending (through equity cash outs etc). And increased thrift will eat into the share of income that is consumed too. So there will be three 'transitional' hits to demand.

The credit bubble was also the mirror and means of financing global imbalances whose genesis was excess consumption (Figure 62).

Part of our thesis is that the resolution of the credit crisis ultimately also addresses the issues of global imbalances. Credit was the means of financing these imbalances (such as the US current account deficit) — remove one and you remove the other.

The decline of the US as a political and economic hegemon will also be a contributor to reducing global imbalances as the US is forced to lower its military pretensions. Lower military spending will mean smaller fiscal deficits to finance. The relative economic decline of the US means that it will act as a weaker magnet for global savings.

Global imbalances have not diminished much yet because there has been a massive credit boost by the monetary and fiscal authorities (mainly in the US) that has sustained these imbalances (Figure 63). As a

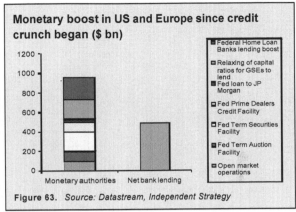

Monetary boost in US and Europe since credit crunch began ($ bn)

Legend:
- Federal Home Loan Banks lending boost
- Relaxing of capital ratios for GSEs to lend
- Fed loan to JP Morgan
- Fed Prime Dealers Credit Facility
- Fed Term Securities Facility
- Fed Term Auction Facility
- Open market operations

Categories: Monetary authorities, Net bank lending

Figure 63. *Source: Datastream, Independent Strategy*

result, the capital allocation system of the US is now more socialised than Hungary's when it was in the Warsaw pact!

But this is just delaying the inevitable. Any return to bull markets based on continued credit expansion by the authorities would not be 'business as usual', but temporary. It would deliver the biggest, shortest boom and bust ever seen.

The end of credit excess

When the crunch is finally over, the next decade will see credit (as measured by the liquidity pyramid) growing much more slowly than during the latter disinflationary decade. It will grow more in line with GDP, or by about 8-10% annually in nominal terms. The trend will be set by a return to prudent lending practices and increased financial sector regulation.

The positive news from this adjustment is that elimination of credit excesses will lead to a better balanced world with more efficient allocation of capital.

What sectors and markets will gain or lose from this world parched of credit?

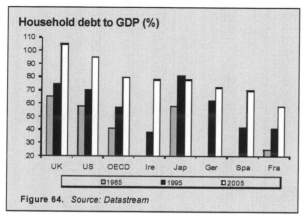

Figure 64. *Source: Datastream*

The gainers would be those economies that have relied on labour productivity growth and incomes from work to sustain growth. That means Germany, Japan and the likes of India.

The most likely losers will be those markets that have been heavily dependent on the housing market bubble and the consumer credit boom (Figure 64). That means the US, the UK, Spain and Ireland. Look for gainers among those who had relied least on these price bubbles, namely Germany, France and Japan.

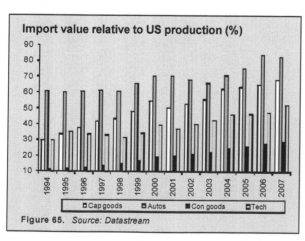

Figure 65. *Source: Datastream*

The sectors that will gain will be US exporters and US companies that benefit from the substitution of local product for imports — namely capital goods and business tech sectors (Figure 65). Elsewhere, it will be European and

Japanese industrials and basic service sectors. The losing sectors are primarily the discretionary consumer goods areas like autos, real estate and finance.

Consumer tamed!

After the credit crunch is resolved, consumption will grow in line with household income not credit supply. Household income expansion will match labour productivity growth more closely. The outperforming markets will again be Germany, Japan, India and parts of Asia. The underperformers will be the US, the UK and non-core Europe.

The sectors to benefit would be consumer staples, basic service sectors like power, telecoms, education and health. The losers would again be consumer discretionary, hi-tech gadgets and luxury goods.

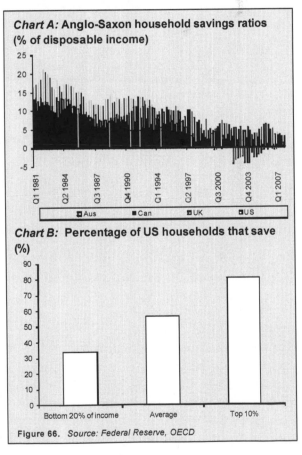

Chart A: Anglo-Saxon household savings ratios (% of disposable income)

Chart B: Percentage of US households that save

Figure 66. *Source: Federal Reserve, OECD*

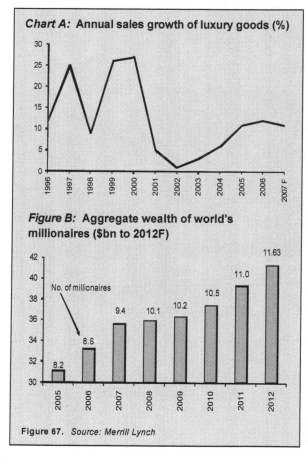

Chart A: Annual sales growth of luxury goods (%)

Figure B: Aggregate wealth of world's millionaires ($bn to 2012F)

Figure 67. *Source: Merrill Lynch*

There will be a return to normal levels of household thrift, particularly in Anglo-Saxon economies (Figure 66). Lower and middle-income groups will be particularly affected and their consumption will grow much more slowly.

The rich, being non-credit shoppers, may continue to consume luxury goods and high-end brands as before, although the number of millionaires in the world is going to grow more slowly (Figure 67).

But the middle- and lower-income groups will return to earth. That means less money on luxury cars, technical gadgets, eating out and expensive foreign holidays. It means more money on basic services, online purchasing and holidays and food at home — and more on saving energy.

End of the Anglo-Saxon Model

The credit crunch is widely perceived as a massive private sector and market failure. The opportunity to grab back power will not be missed by politicians and bureaucrats.

The end of credit excesses will vitiate to some degree Anglo-Saxon *laissez faire* economic policies as the universally accepted paradigm. There will be greater regulation of the financial sector. But increased state intervention won't stop there. Both climate change and a globally fragile food supply chain may also result in greater government intervention.

Three flaws in the Anglo Saxon model are now obvious in hindsight and will result in a political shift towards a more interventionist and redistributive state.

The first flaw was to make housing affordable for people who shouldn't ever have owned houses. These are now an economically-dispossessed cohort of the US population, many of them belonging to Afro-American and Hispanic ethnic groups (Figure 68).

This will have political implications for markets and international free trade when the Democrats, for whom the dispossessed vote (if they vote), come to power. They stand for more regulation, trade protection and subsidies.

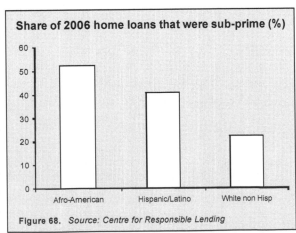

Figure 68. *Source: Centre for Responsible Lending*

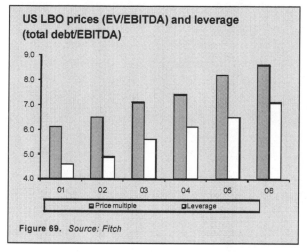

US LBO prices (EV/EBITDA) and leverage (total debt/EBITDA)

Price multiple   Leverage

Figure 69. *Source: Fitch*

The second flaw was to boost asset values by engineering corporate deals that created wealth for the few (investors) but added no value to the consumer of the product (e.g. LBOs of airlines that created bigger and lousier entities) — Figure 69.

The third flaw was to promote extreme wealth and income differentials between people in the real economy (particularly those doing solidly virtuous jobs like teachers, policemen and nurses) and financial sector employees and leaders (Figure 70).

Since the 1980s, the share of net worth for the wealthiest 20% of US households has increased (Figure 70A). Their share has been rising at over 2% a year, while the median US household has seen no improvement since the 1990s (Figure 70B). The wealthiest Americans have nearly 200 times more wealth than the average American, up 25% since the early 1980s (Figure 70C). And the Gini coefficient, a measure of income inequality, has risen the most in the last 20 years in the 'financial centre' countries of the US and the UK (Figure 70D).

The financiers have now been proven grossly wanting in the basic financial skills, like risk assessment, they were supposed to be expert in using to create unprecedented wealth for the relatively few and privileged.

The political shift that all of this will empower is a return to bigger and more interventionist (as well as income and wealth-redistributive) government. There will be higher corporate taxes and lower profit shares in national income. And of course there will be more regulation, particularly of the financial sector. The wealthy will see their tax burden rise.

Profit and wage shares will reverse trend as a proportion of national income with wages expanding and profits shrinking. Low growth in productivity and a wage catch-up will ensure this happens through higher inflation. This means much lower real profit growth going forward.

However, reported profits will, in other ways, be healthier. Corporate asset values will be set by fundamentals (present value of future income) and not financial engineering. They will be cheaper. M&A strategy will

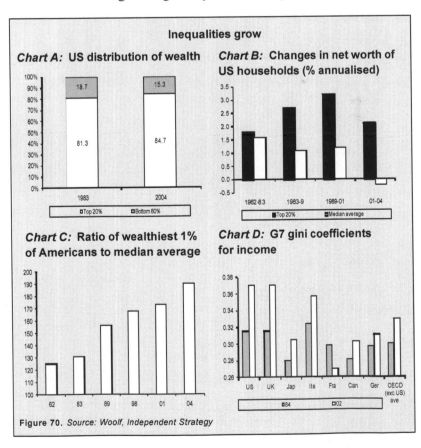

Figure 70. Source: Woolf, Independent Strategy

become less of an MBA-whiz-kid strategy and more driven by corporate logic.

There will be something of a rebirth of the staid (but safe and balanced) European social market model affecting many sectors. For example, the Eurozone and Japanese universal banking model, with its greater reliance on relationship-oriented banking and based on a much higher degree of banking intermediation between saving and investment (Figure 71), has proven to be much more stable in crisis than the Anglo-Saxon model of credit origination, securitisation and distribution (COD) — Figure 72.

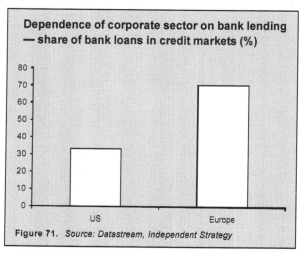

Figure 71. *Source: Datastream, Independent Strategy*

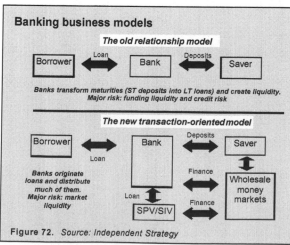

Figure 72. *Source: Independent Strategy*

The usual argument against Europe and Japan's revival is that these are 'old' countries with a rapidly aging population and low labour participation compared to the US and other 'Anglo-Saxon' economies. But youthful demographics are not decisive. If they were, then Africa would be booming and China slowing fast. Indeed, a youthful population (Africa and the Middle East) is more associated with underdevelopment than creativity and productivity gains.

Moreover, an ageing population concentrates the minds of politicians in Europe and Japan on the need to reform pensions and social security programees and to run balanced budgets. It also focuses the minds of employers on compensating for increasingly scarce labour with more creative and productive use of it.

So there's a big short/long trade between those markets that are forced to break with the Anglo-Saxon model like the US and the UK and those that have not had asset-price bubbles fuelled by cheap credit and the property bubble (Germanic Europe and Japan).

The sectors to benefit are manufacturing, capital goods and infrastructure along with safe money tax havens and gold.

Disinflation soooo dead!

The disinflationary period is dead. In fact, it died some time ago (Figure 73)! It will be replaced by a period of widely differentiated inflation rates in different economic blocs. Europe will remain the world's low inflation anchor with strong currencies (euro and swissie) to match, followed by Japan.

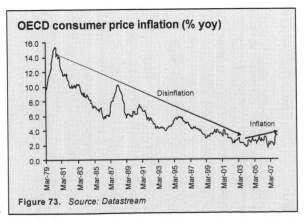

Figure 73. Source: Datastream

The US will continue to pursue easy-option policies to soften the blow from the credit crisis and

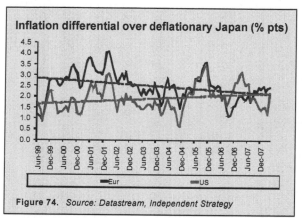

Figure 74. *Source: Datastream, Independent Strategy*

prioritise growth over inflation. "Acceptable" higher underlying inflation rates (3-5%) will be targeted in the US, tolerated in Japan and rejected by the ECB (Figure 74).

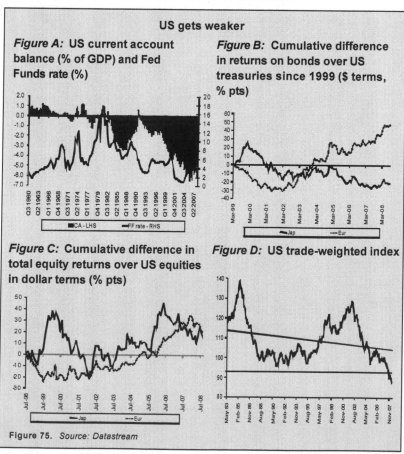

Figure 75. *Source: Datastream*

The US will suffer relative economic decline as a consequence. The perceived weakness of the US, already evident for some years in financial markets, will mean foreigners will be increasingly reluctant to finance the US external deficit and will only do so for higher reward.

This will have three consequences (Figure 75). First, the US current account will adjust downwards as the financing of it becomes more costly and cautious. This means structurally higher US long-term interest rates and, consequently mediocre US consumption and investment growth for a lengthy period (Figure 75A).

Second, US financial assets will continue to underperform their global peers (Figures 75B and 75C). Third, the US dollar will remain the world's weakest major currency for several years, despite the gradual shrinkage in the current account deficit (Figure 75D).

Emerging markets and global inflation

Emerging markets will become a source of global inflation rather than disinflation (see Figure 76 on page 94), as is already starting to happen. Asia and Latin America are now net contributors to global inflation (Figure 76A).

Like the US, most emerging markets will pursue soft options when their economies turn down, in particular by having their currencies shadow the sick US dollar (Figure 76B) or be even weaker than it. This will slow the improvement in the US trade imbalance and add to emerging market domestic inflation.

The globalised forces of technology, trade and monetary disinflation that held emerging market inflation down as much as it did for rich countries are all waning (Figures 76C and 76D).

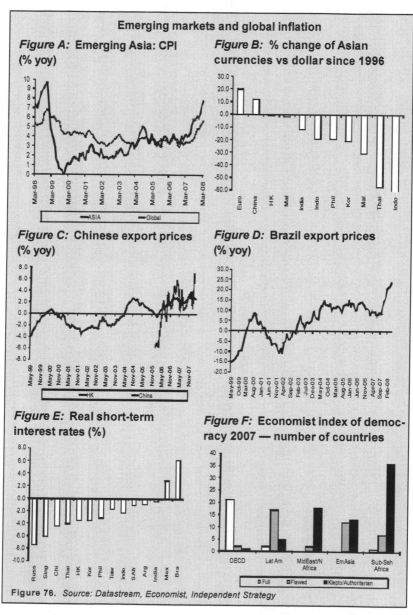

Figure 76. *Source: Datastream, Economist, Independent Strategy*

Emerging markets, with rare exceptions like Brazil, Mexico and India, lack independent, tough, central banks to control inflation (Figure 76E).

And finally, ironically, dictatorships and corrupt klepto-democracies in emerging markets cannot bear economic pain to the degree that rich democracies can (Figure 76F).

Inflation and investment

In the next decade, OECD inflation will be closer to 4% than 2%. The causes of this upward shift will be sloppy central banking in the US; emerging market inflation; and ongoing global food (but not energy and industrial commodity) inflation (Figure 77). Above all, there will be a global wage catch-up (Figure 78), eroding corporate profit margins. The wage catch-up will be more severe in emerging markets where living standards have suffered more from rising food and energy prices than in OECD countries.

Higher inflation and bigger government in a low-growth environment is very bad news for government bonds, with the relative winner being the Eurozone. US treasuries, the greenback and the mini-dollar bloc are shorts, as are sterling and gilts.

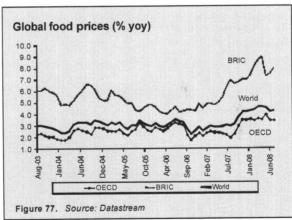

Global food prices (% yoy)

Figure 77. *Source: Datastream*

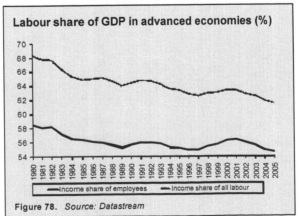

Labour share of GDP in advanced economies (%)

Figure 78. *Source: Datastream*

Macro and financial indicators in selected Emerging Market countries (estimates for 2007 to April 2008)

The IMF has done a study of a range of vulnerabilities that would make emerging markets susceptible to any deterioration in the external environment (namely a global credit crunch). The IMF reckons that any emerging market with more than a 5% of GDP current account deficit; private sector credit growth of more than 20% in 2007-8; growth in ratio of credit to GDP of more than 10% pts; and net liabilities to foreign banks of more than 10% of GDP would be vulnerable to economic recession or financial collapse. If you add fiscal balances to the equation (deficit greater than 2%), again the same countries look weak. The emerging markets that qualify on four or more counts include Bulgaria, Romania and the Baltic states. Turkey and Kazakhstan also score badly.

Figure 79. *Source: IMF*

Among sectors, food and gold will be outperformers, along with TIPS and other inflation-indexed bonds, as well as yield steepener trades, particularly in the US and the UK.

In a lower growth, more protectionist world, the strongest emerging markets will be those able to promote non-inflationary domestic demand without credit excesses, while maintaining balanced external and fiscal accounts (Figure 79). That would be Asia over Latin America and Emerging Europe, in that order.

Investors will also reward those markets where central banks are tough on inflation. Judged

Current average real policy interest rates by region (%)

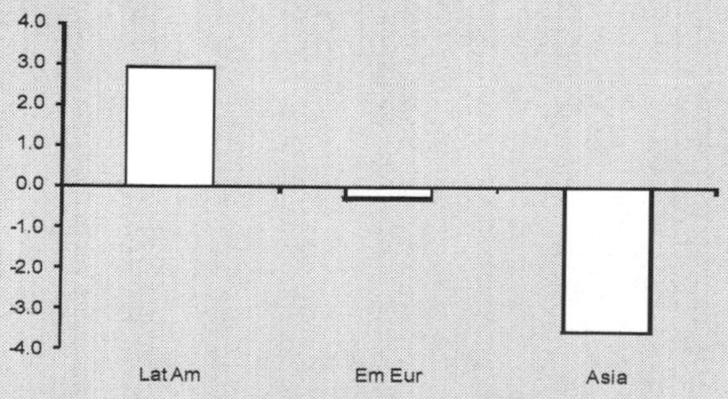

Figure 80. *Source: Datastream*

by the level of real policy rates, Latin America has performed the best (and will continue to do so if market anticipations are right) and Asia the worst (Figure 80).

One challenge will be to raise labour productivity to afford higher income per capita. In emerging markets, risk capital will flow to where growth is strongest, domestic credit ratios are reasonable and where current account balances show the biggest <u>marginal</u> improvement.

World trade and EM societal crux points

World trade will grow more slowly due to the lack of excess consumption in developed countries. Successful emerging markets will switch to increasingly domestically-oriented growth policies.

This inevitably goes together with the emergence or strengthening of a property-owning middle class that will prioritise protection of its economic and civil rights to a much greater degree than when these economies were emerging from poverty and dictatorship. That creates the political demand for a civic and legal society.

Societal development will be key in achieving this; it is no coincidence that all countries that are advanced economies are also democracies founded on the rule of law. This is because competition in one area drives competition in the other.

In Asia the societal/economic development pecking order is currently reversed: dictatorships lead democracies (e.g. China versus India) in economic development (Figure 81). But this is not the advent of a new paradigm, but a momentary stage of economic development in political autarchies,

India versus China	China	India
Poverty (% below $1 a day)	10.8	35.1
Human development index	0.768	0.611
Tertiary education share (%)	21	13
GDP per unit of energy use	4.4	5.5
Daily protein consumption (gm epr cap)	91	63
Life expectancy	74	59
Per cap GNI ($)	1740	730

Figure 81. *Source: World Bank*

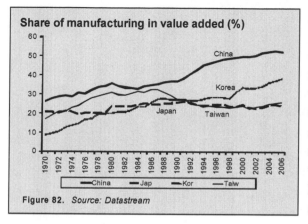

Figure 82. *Source: Datastream*

matched by excessive household and corporate savings rates and over-investment in tradable goods as well as an "export or die" economic development model. Both have finite advantages for economic develop-ment that are currently being reached in China.

The China model mirrors that of Japan, Taiwan and Korea at an earlier stage of industrialisation, but has gone on far longer and is now past its use-by-date (Figure 82).

The next stage of emerging market development means taking a big risk on societal political liberalisation at the same time as developing a middle-class consumer and service economy. India and Korea are much more likely to make this leap than China, the Philippines or Indonesia. The sectors that will outperform in emerging markets that successfully trans-form themselves are consumer sectors, real estate and services such as health and education.

Climate change, resource competition and food

The latest scientific evidence suggests that damage from climate change will happen more rapidly and more catastrophically than forecast. Poli-cies to deal with the potential threat and its actual consequences will become embedded and non-cyclical. While market-based systems, such as carbon trading, may dominate the mitigation process, direct government intervention to regulate emissions will bolster the interventionist role of the state in the economy in general and create greater public acceptance of it.

Carbon emissions will be regulated globally with the participation of the US, India and China in the next "Kyoto" accord. Non-participating states will encounter eco-protectionism forcing them to do so.

The key economic impact of climate change will be on food. Although still subject to the 'hog cycle', food price inflation will remain high due to supply constraints (mainly due to eco-damage) and continued growth in demand for decent (clean) food in newly industrialised countries that have destroyed the ability to produce their own supply.

The gap between growth in supply and demand is already in evidence. According to the OECD and FAO, between 2005-7, production of cereals rose 3% and demand by 5%. In vegetable oils, the growth gap was also 2% pts.

In the future, apart from normal hog-cycle reversals causing food prices to dip temporarily, the growing gap between demand and supply will make food price inflation and supply shortage a recurrent feature on the macro landscape. The result will be to raise structural inflation rates in many emerging markets, lessening their impact as a global disninflationary force.

Geopolitical tensions due to climate change will increase eco-diaspora; "have versus have-nots" terrorism; and competition and conflict for land and water. Indeed, water management will become a major economic and investment issue.

Global trade in agricultural products will continue to grow rapidly, despite increased political intervention to protect domestic food autonomy. It has

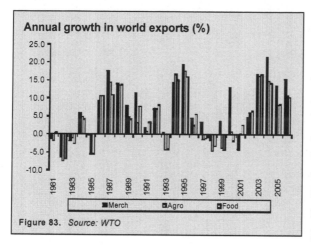

Annual growth in world exports (%)

Figure 83. *Source: WTO*

been growing at double-digits for the last five years — the longest such run on record (Figure 83). There is a long way to go. Only 10% of coarse grain, 18% of wheat and less than 10% of rice production are traded internationally. These ratios will probably rise towards 40% in the next decade.

Those with a comparative advantage in food production will boom. This will embrace African and Eastern Europe countries as well as Latin America (Figure 84). However, some naturally endowed agricultural producers, like Argentina, will destroy these advantages through bad governance and a lack of social coherence.

There will be some surprise new agricultural super-producers that have not yet figured on the investment radar screen (like Ukraine and Southern Africa). There are opportunities for investment in these new producers through private equity and funds.

Hard commodities and oil

The prices of hard commodities, and to a lesser extent energy, have been driven to astronomical levels by two factors: speculation and the China (i.e. big emerging market development) story.

China's burgeoning demand for these resources is at least partly down to substitution of 'resource wasting' production in China for 'resource economic' production outside China. This transfer of production was implemented through FDI.

The economic equation that made China competitive despite inefficient resource utilisation was its comparative advantage in labour, where its costs dwarfed the cost of inefficient use of capital, energy and raw materials (Figure 85).

China's demography, even over the next ten years, indicates that its "endless" supply of cheap labour is finite (Figure 86).

This will cause China's wage costs to rise rapidly relative to its trading partners and even relative to

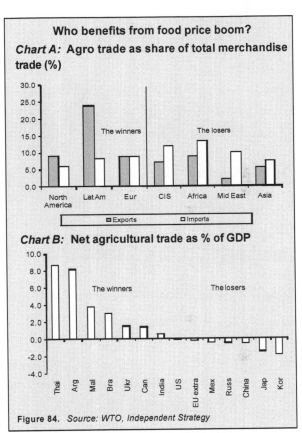

Who benefits from food price boom?

Chart A: **Agro trade as share of total merchandise trade (%)**

The winners / The losers

□ Exports   □ Imports

Chart B: **Net agricultural trade as % of GDP**

The winners / The losers

Figure 84. *Source: WTO, Independent Strategy*

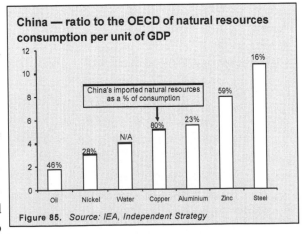

China — ratio to the OECD of natural resources consumption per unit of GDP

China's imported natural resources as a % of consumption

Oil 46% · Nickel 28% · Water N/A · Copper 80% · Aluminium 23% · Zinc 59% · Steel 16%

Figure 85. *Source: IEA, Independent Strategy*

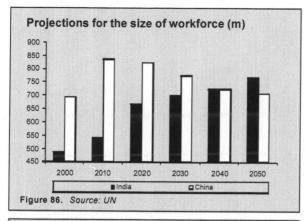

Figure 86. *Source: UN*

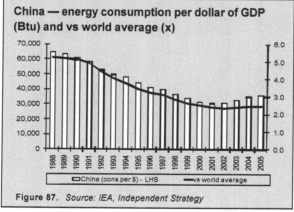

Figure 87. *Source: IEA, Independent Strategy*

competitive EM producers, such as India, whose demographics are much more favourable.

The result is that China's period of export-led super growth will end because of gradually fading wage competitiveness; and more immediately, because of elimination of excess US consumption growth.

As China's exports shrink, so will upstream excess demand for commodities and speculative investment in them. China's use of hard commodities and energy will also become more efficient as domestic prices converge with global ones making wastage expensive (Figure 87).

Prices of hard commodities will again start to reflect the shrinking proportion they represent of global output and a sub-global GDP growth rate going forward.

Supply of industrial materials, boosted by the euphoria of the boom years, will rapidly surpass actual and prospective multi-year growth in demand (Figure 88). The classic down-cycle in industrial commodity prices will have begun! Oil, despite its opaque and politicised supply curve will also see its price fall to the mid-$50s per barrel.

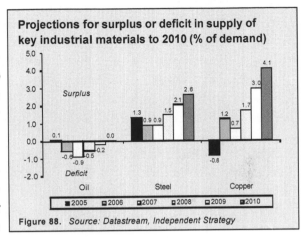

Projections for surplus or deficit in supply of key industrial materials to 2010 (% of demand)

Figure 88. *Source: Datastream, Independent Strategy*

The return to reality will be financially painful for investors. But the decline in energy and commodity prices will be helpful in containing inflation and keeping the world growing. And it will take the swagger out of alternative politics in certain Latin American countries and in Russia. Declining oil and commodity revenues will reduce the impact of sovereign wealth funds and transfer those 'savings' to higher thrift in OECD households and thus 'normalise' financial markets.

In a lower growth world, those emerging markets that depend on the export of oil and metals rather than food will struggle. That means Russia, Venezuela and Nigeria. The winners are Brazil, Argentina, Ukraine, Vietnam, Thailand, Australia and New Zealand.

Geopolitics

Coincidentally, the US started to lose economic clout and global leadership with the first election of the second President George Bush. But the underlying reasons were the development of patterns of behaviour that characterised other empires at their zenith and turning points.

These include over-consumption at the core of the empire relative to its ability to produce, over reliance on the contribution of the periphery to finance the core's excesses and imbalances and over-confidence in the economic model and the ability of the empire to project power.

The bursting of the credit bubble and the seeming inability of the US authorities to deal with the consequences in an orthodox (if painful) manner, will result in another step-down in US power.

That will not create the multipolar world that many fear, with China and Russia snapping at the heels of a jaded US. Nor does it herald a world in which medium-size powers compete for global resources using military force (there are few recidivist claims that matter on a global scale and the world's scarce resources can no longer be captured by colonisation).

Instead, it will be much more of a cooperative world without a dominant power, though the US will remain the single most powerful state, where much will be decided by haggling and conflicts will be resolved by compromise — much like the EU today. That is not necessarily a bad thing. It can lead to a stable, secular, non-ideological global comity with characteristics quite similar to a community of middle-class states.

CHAPTER TEN

Coconut Island —
New Monetarism on a desert island

There was this desert island that produced coconuts. The inhabitants ate them to survive. Any surplus they sold to passing boats, putting the money they got under their mattresses for a rainy day (very rare) and to buy luxuries and tools (from yet other passing boats).

Alas, the islanders never had enough money to find more water and plant more coconut trees. One day along came some gal in a pirogue who founded a bank. This was the Coconut Island's first bank. The bank paid interest on savings deposited with it. So everyone rushed to deposit their mattress money in the bank.

Before long, there were several banks, even some started by men. Together, they were able to lend far more money than the initial deposits. Every time they lent out money, a fairly high proportion ended up being redeposited back in the banks after being used to pay for more coconut trees, wells and houses. But there was a big change. The inhabitants were able to borrow enough from the banks to grow more trees and, later, to build proper houses for themselves.

Every coconut tree cost 100 widgits (w), including the land to grow it on and earned 8w a year. As the island had a government of sorts, there were taxes of 25%. Interest on borrowings was 4% and tax deductible. These were the only cash costs as everyone tended their own trees.

Balance sheet (w)

	With banks			Before banks
Assets			**Assets**	
Palm trees X 2 =	200		Palm tree X 1 =	100
Liabilities			**Liabilities**	
Bank debt =	100		Bank Debt =	0
Equity =	100		Equity =	100
Total =	200		Total =	100
P&L account (w):				
Revenues			**Revenues**	
Coconut sales	16		Coconut sales	8
Expenses			**Expenses**	
Interest at 4%:	4		Interest:	0
Pre-tax profit	12		Pre-tax profit	8
Tax at 25%:	3		Tax at 25%:	2
After-tax profit	9		After-tax profit	6

Figure 89. *Source: Independent Strategy*

Most farmers started life with one palm tree. But since the advent of banks they could then borrow 100w to buy another. So an individual farmer's balance sheet and profit and loss statement would look like Figure 89.

It was clear to all that the coming of the banks and the creation of credit had made everyone richer. Now everyone earned 9w a year. Previously, everyone in coconuts earned only 6w. And real productive capacity had doubled, as everyone now had two trees instead of one.

The along came some "smart" young people. People knew they were smart because they had Blackberries, laptops and dark glasses. People knew they were rich (and therefore smart) because they came in a speedboat.

They did not want to tend palm trees. In reality, the newcomers were beach bums. They intended to spend the day surfing and chatting up maidens in bars, which the island's new-found prosperity had made possible, so increasing GDP, sexual disease, unwanted sprogs and unhappiness in one fell swoop. However, all of this cost money. The issue was how to get it.

The beach bums decided to buy 50% of one producer of palm trees. This would cost 60w as the farmer wanted to make more money than it had cost him to set up the business. And it would entitle the beach bums to the income of one of the two palm trees that the farmer would continue to tend as part of the deal.

Then the beach bums went to one of the banks and borrowed 50w and put down 10w of their own money and called their new company PCE, standing for the Private (Coconut) Equity Fund. The PCE balance sheet would now look like Figure 90.

Everyone lived happily afterwards. The beach bums earned a 45% return on their equity. The farmer still earned a good living and had an extra 60w to play with. And he still earned a net 2w from his remaining palm tree (revenues 8w less interest 4w and tax 2w = 2w).

Balance sheet (w)	
Assets	
50% of 1 Coconut enterprise =	60
Liabilities	
Bank debt	50
Equity	10
Total	60
The P&L looked like this:	
Revenues	
Coconut sales	8
Expenses	
Interest at 4%	2
Pre-tax profit	6
Tax at 25%	1.5
After-tax profit	4.5
Return on equity (4.5w/10w = 45%)	

Figure 90. *Source: Independent Strategy*

Then along came another set of beach bums, in a chopper this time, with much the same ambitions as their peers. Alas, there were no more coconut enterprises for sale (everyone was hanging out for higher prices after the first deal became known).

But they had a new idea. Instead of buying a coconut enterprise, the new beach bums took themselves off to the bank and said "we want to buy half of your loan book (=150w, of which 100w are for loans to palm tree owners and 50w to PCE) at book value".

The bank manager thought this was a good idea because he could use the new money to make more loans, this time for home finance that paid 7% instead of 4%. And anyway, he didn't like the coconut business so much any more and wanted to diversify his loan book. Moreover, he could lend the new set of beach bums 90% of the cost of the loan book they were buying, which he offered at 3% — the current short-term bank rate.

But the beach bums were international players and they said 'no thanks' to the loan by the local bank. Instead, they rang their Japanese bank (although none of them was Japanese). The Japanese bank lent them the money based on Japanese market rates currently standing at 0.25% for three years. The rate of interest was adjustable quarterly. But the beach bums didn't worry about the variable interest rate as they could lock in that rate for three years by buying interest-rate options (derivatives).

So the second set of beach bums set up a company called CCDO, standing for Collateralised Coconut Debt Obligations. Their financial statements read happily too as in Figure 91.

They earned a 28% return on their equity. The banker was happy. He was able to lend an extra 75w for housing (which caused the island's real estate to rise in price by 25% in the following months). This not only diversified his business, but increased the average interest yield on his loan book from 4% to 5.5%. His gross interest income (upon which his bonus was based) jumped by 37.5% (from 6w to 8.25w).

Balance sheet (w)	
Assets	
Loans (50% of the banks' outstanding loans of 150)	75
Liabilities	
Bank debt	67.5
Equity	7.5
Total	75
The P&L looked like this:	
Revenues	
Interest income (75 at 4%)	3
Expenses	
Interest (67.5 at 0.25%)	0.2
Pre-tax profit	2.8
Tax at 25%	0.7
After-tax profit	2.1
Return on equity (2.1w/7.5w = 28%)	

Figure 91. *Source: Independent Strategy*

The island's people were happy because they felt, and were, richer. House prices soared. Foreign yen inflows had made the widget strong. So everyone could afford a holiday in Miami. In fact, people felt so good that they started to put less money aside for a rainy day. After all, why should they save? Rising asset prices meant that their houses and palm trees kept making them richer while they slept. And the government was happy because it made lots more tax from increased profits and real estate taxes.

COCONUT ISLAND

Balance sheet (w)

Assets

2 x Palm trees   200

Liabilities   292.5
(original bank debt 100w + PCE debt
50w + CCDO debt 67.5w + housing
debt 75w)

Net worth   (92.5)

Figure 92. *Source: Independent Strategy*

So everyone was happy, except for one old guy who lived on the beach and owned no home and no palm tree. He pointed out that only the original loan had created real wealth by doubling coconut capacity in which it was invested. All the rest was just a layering of debt on an unchanged productive asset.

He drew a T account in the sand. He said it represented the real balance sheet of the island, as in Figure 92.

So he said to those who would listen: " you may feel rich. But it is only asset price inflation and debt that makes you think so. Instead you are bankrupt. Because even your houses are worthless if the trees stop producing nuts". But then the happy blue tide rose and the rippling waters washed away his writing and any trace of concern in the mind of his audience...

Until one horrible day, when the price of coconuts fell 25% and the bank doubled the cost of lending because no-one was saving any more and inflation had reached 5%, meaning it had to charge 7% on all loans. You can work the balance sheets backwards yourself to see they do not balance any more!

Bibliography

Bank of International Settlements, Quarterly reviews, *www.bis.org*

Bank of International Settlements, *The global OTC derivatives market,* end December 2006

IMF, World Economic Outlooks, *www.imf.org*

IMF, Global financial stability bi-annuals, *www.imf.org*

International Swaps and Derivatives Association, *www.isda.org*

US Comptroller of the Currency, quarterly derivatives fact sheets, *www.occ.treas.gov/deriv/deriv.htm*

Federal Bank of New York, Current issues in economics and finance, December 2006, (Matthew Higgins, Thomas Klitgaard and Robert Lerman), *Recycling petrodollars; www.newyorkfed.org*

Ben S. Bernanke, Homer Jones Lecture, 14 April 2005: *The global saving glut and the US current account deficit, www.federalreserve.gov/boarddocs/speeches/2005/20050414/ default.htm*

Ben S. Bernanke, Brian P. Sack, and Vincent R. Reinhart, Brookings Papers on Economic Analysis (2004), *Monetary Policy Alternatives at the Zero Bound: An Empirical Assessment; www.brook.edu*

Hernando de Soto, *The mystery of capital,* Bantam Press, 2000

Claudio Borio and Philip Lowe, BIS Working paper No 114, July 2002, *Asset prices, financial and monetary stability: exploring the nexus*

William White, <u>BIS working paper 205, April 2006</u>: *Is price stability enough?*

Michael Bordo, <u>IMF World Economic Outlook, April 2003,</u> p64 Box 2.1: *When bubbles burst*

Kunio Okina and Shigenori Shiratsuka, <u>Monetary and Economic Studies,</u> Institute for Monetary and Economic Studies, Bank of Japan, vol. 20(3), pages 35-76, October 2002, *Asset price bubbles, price stability and monetary policy: Japan's experience*

Robert Shiller, *www.econ.yale.edu/~shiller/*

James Tobin, <u>Journal of Money Credit and Banking</u>, Vol 1No 1 pp 15-29. (1969) *A general equilibrium approach to monetary theory*

Andrew Smithers and Stephen Wright, *Valuing Wall street: protecting wealth in turbuluent markets* McGraw-Hill, 2000

Charles Kindleberger, *Manias, panics and crashes — a history of financial crashes,* 2000

Hyman Minsky, in Kindleberger and Laffargue, editors: <u>Financial Crises, 1982;</u> *The financial-instability hypothesis: capitalist processes and the behaviour of the economy*

New York Federal Reserve and Princeton University, Tobias Adrian and Hyun Sing, *Liquidity and leverage, September 2007*

Federal Reserve Board, <u>2007-47</u>, Michael Gibson, *Credit derivatives and risk management*

Fitch Ratings, September 2006, *Credit derivatives survey;* July 2007, *CDX survey*

US Monetary Policy Forum, February 2008, *Leveraged losses: lessons from the mortgage market meltdown*

Carol Corrado, Charles Hulten, Daniel Sichel, Federal Reserve Board, October 2005, *Intangible capital and economic growth*